Stay Close: 40 Clever Ways to Connect with Kids When You're Apart

"Divorce separates parents from children so that they may no longer wake up and be in the same house with them. Tenessa Gemelke provides unique, practical ways to stay connected in *Stay Close*. It's the divorced parent's answer to bridging the in-between time with their children."

Dr. David Knox, author of *The Divorced Dad's Survival Book*

• • • • •

"Here's a book you'll want to keep out and refer to again and again to spark that 'next idea' for keeping in touch with kids."

Vicki Lansky, author of *101 Ways to Make Your Child Feel Special*, and *Vicki Lansky's Divorce Book for Parents*

• • • • •

"If you want to stay connected to a young person you love but do not live with, *Stay Close* is the book for you. . . . It will encourage you, teach you, and get you started down the path of a relationship that might just last a lifetime."

William C. Klatte, author of *Live-Away Dads*

"Well written, and offering dozens of practical suggestions . . . *Stay Close* is an important new contribution to the literature on building healthy interpersonal relationships, whether at a long, or short distance."

Selma Wasserman, author of *The Long Distance Grandmother*

•   •   •   •   •

"As a passionate grandparent, of course my heart's desire is to stay connected with this flesh of my flesh of my flesh. . . . But *how* when so many miles separate us? After reading the clever, inspired and specific ideas presented in *Stay Close*, I feel armed, relaxed, confident, and fret free. I'll be recommending this book as often as I recommend my own!"

—Charlene Ann Baumbich, author of *365 Ways to Connect With Your Kids No Matter What Their Age [Or Yours]* and *Don't Miss Your Kids! (they'll be gone before you know it*

STAY CLOSE

STAY CLOSE

Clever Ways to Connect with Kids When You're Apart

TENESSA GEMELKE

A SEARCH INSTITUTE PUBLICATION

Search
INSTITUTE

Practical research
benefiting children
and youth

Stay Close: 40 Clever Ways to Connect
with Kids When You're Apart
Tenessa Gemelke

Copyright © 2005 by Search Institute
Search Institute^{SM} and Developmental Assets™ are trademarks of Search Institute.

At the time of publication, all facts and figures cited herein are the most current available; all telephone numbers, addresses, and Web site URLs are accurate and active; all publications, organizations, Web sites, and other resources exist as described in this book; and all efforts have been made to verify them. The author and Search Institute make no warranty or guarantee concerning the information and materials given out by organizations or content found at Web sites that are cited herein, and we are not responsible for any changes that occur after this book's publication. If you find an error or believe that a resource listed herein is not as described, please contact Client Services at Search Institute.

ISBN-13: 978-1-57482-870-2
ISBN-10: 1-57482-870-3

Library of Congress Cataloging-in-Publication Data
    Stay close : 40 clever ways to connect with kids when you're apart /
Tenessa Gemelke.
        p. cm.
    Includes bibliographical references.
    ISBN 1-57482-870-3 (paperbook : alk. paper)
    1. Children—Family relationships. 2. Children and adults.
3. Interpersonal relations in children. 4. Interpersonal communication
in children. 5. Interpersonal communication in adolescence. I. Title.

HQ767.9.G45 2005
646.7'8—dc22   2005012498

10 9 8 7 6 5 4 3 2 1
Printed on acid-free paper in Canada.

Search Institute
615 First Avenue NE, Suite 125
Minneapolis, MN 55413
www.search-institute.org
612-376-8955 • 800-888-7828

Credits
Editor: Anitra Budd, Ruth Taswell
Book Design: Percolator
Production Coordinator: Mary Ellen Buscher

*For Weldon "Bill" Garrison, Jeannette Gemelke,
and the late Robert Gemelke, the three best
grandparents a kid ever had*

and

*For Linus Gemelke Lee, whose birth has made me
happier than I knew I could be.*

Contents

A Knock at the Door

Now That We're Together

Don't Be a Stranger

Acknowledgments

I suppose the downfall of being an editor is that I know how *many* individuals contribute to the publication of a single book. Because I run the risk of thanking far too many people, I'll start by saying that my family, my friends, and my colleagues at Search Institute gave me tremendous support as I researched and wrote this book. I am grateful to you all.

Having said that, I do wish to express special gratitude to several people.

I thank my two editors: Ruth Taswell gave me early encouragement and support getting the project off the ground, and Anitra Budd offered wisdom, talent, and tireless optimism in the face of a wild schedule. I thank Kay Hong and Kathleen Kimball-Baker for believing in me and giving me the chance to write this book.

I'd like to thank the people who converted the manuscript into a real, live book: Mary Ellen Buscher is an outstanding production coordinator, and she showed genuine enthusiasm for this topic. Brad Boettcher and Mark Reis at Percolator are fantastic designers and were incredibly helpful when we made last-minute changes to the cover.

You'll see several names mentioned in anecdotes throughout the book. These people were all kind enough to share their stories about long-distance families and friendships. I am also grateful to Mary Ackerman, Karen Bartig, Jim Conway, Phillip Donlay, Stephanie Drakulich, Betsy Gabler, Jennifer Ganyo, Kristin Green, Sandra Harris, Pat

Howell-Blackmore, Bill Kauffman, Dave Lee, Cora Mc-Michael, Gladys Roth, Susanne Smith, Terri Swanson, and Nancy Tellet-Royce for reading the first draft and giving their valuable suggestions for improving it.

I thank my family for teaching me the value of staying in touch across distances. I know how challenging it is as an auntie to five far-away nieces and nephews, and I have to confess the irony that I managed to be exceptionally late sending *two* of them birthday presents while writing this book! Staying close is hard work, but they've taught me that it's definitely worthwhile.

Finally, I offer deepest thanks to my husband, my dad, and my baby; these guys fed me, loved me, and gave me time to write in peace at home. I couldn't have done it without them.

Far Away but
Not Distant

Each year when my brother and I received our JCPenney gift certificates from Grandpa Bill, we knew Christmas had truly arrived. We'd spend hours poring over the catalog, memorizing every page in the toy section. Some years, we would combine our finances for a bigger purchase; other years, we would guard every penny for personal indulgences. Even though our grandfather couldn't always be with us for the holidays, this yearly ritual gave him a memorable place in our young lives.

Grandpa Bill lived in Michigan and Arizona, and he enjoyed traveling to other places as well. He was always great about sending postcards to us in Minnesota. We had lived near him when we were very young, but we only saw him once or twice a year throughout much of our childhood. His annual Christmas gesture was a token of his permanence. It showed us we could always count on our grandpa.

The funny thing is, I no longer recall the dollar amount of the gift certificates, and I can only remember one or two items I chose to buy. What I do remember is the anticipation, the pride in making my own decision, and the gratitude I felt afterward. It was the gesture and the tradition that mattered. Because of this, and so many other efforts over the years, I knew my grandfather cared about me. He and I still have a very close relationship to this day.

You may live or travel far away from your children, grandchildren, stepchildren, nieces, nephews, or family friends, but you have the capacity to give them a valuable gift: yourself! Being apart presents a number of unique challenges, but in these pages you'll find anecdotes, resources, and creative strategies for bridging the distance—geographical and emotional—that often separates young people from the adults who care about them.

IS THIS BOOK FOR ME?

Distance keeps us from loved ones due to a variety of circumstances. A wonderful job opportunity may involve business travel for a parent. Close friends might settle in communities at opposite ends of the continent, where they have few opportunities to spend time with each other's children. Military deployment can force parents to live apart from their children for months at a time. Seniors may relocate far away from their extended families after retirement. Some families struggle with the painful challenges of divorce, estrangement, or even incarceration. When you list these obstacles, you begin to see that distance, in all its forms, is a common and widespread problem in modern life.

Kriss Johnson understands the difficulties of separation firsthand. When she describes her childhood as a "military brat" moving around the United States, she warmly recalls the stability of her grandparents' home in Florida. Later, when the topic turns to her divorce as an adult, she expresses regret about the time she lost with her two teenage sons after she moved from their home in North Dakota to California. Today, Kriss lives in Georgia, and she is the adoring grandmother of a little girl and a little boy who live in two different states. Even one person's story can show numerous ways young people are separated from the adults who care about them.

Many obstacles may keep you apart from one or more young people in your life—but what keeps you *close?* The answer is simple: commitment. Your decision to pick up this book and take action shows you are ready to conquer the difficulties of geographic distance and foster a loving relationship across the miles. Your goal is possible and doable, and the rewards are great. This book *is* for you.

GROWING, GROWING . . . GONE?

As if the distance wasn't enough, you may also find yourself stunned by how quickly kids change. The infant who snuggled in your lap is now a boisterous 7-year-old. The preschooler who gave you artwork for the refrigerator is suddenly an awfully shy teenager. Even if you were once closely connected to these kids, an increasing lack of familiarity and new feelings of awkwardness on both sides can arise as the years go by.

Whether you are starting from scratch or rekindling a once-fond relationship, it is important to adjust your approach to the young person's age and maturity level. Some of the ideas in this book will work better with younger children, and others will appeal to the preferences of older teens. Many of the activities include variations to make ideas accessible and interesting to kids of all ages.

If you do strike out with one idea, step back up to the plate. A failed connection can be disappointing, but when you remain flexible and optimistic, you are more likely to find an opportunity that works well for both the young person and you.

WHO'S GOING TO PAY FOR ALL THIS?

I once met a woman who described a strict rule for first dates: The entire date must cost no more than five dollars. She said that too often people spend so much time eating dinner and watching a movie that they never really get to know each other. Her tiny budget was just enough for bus fare or coffee, and she had some wonderful dates at parks, public art exhibits, and beaches. Good conversation doesn't cost a thing.

Long-distance relationships can seem even more dependent on money than dates. Each change in technology comes with a price tag, and you may feel out of touch if you don't have voice messaging, text messaging, and instant messaging. While a lack of money and electronic gadgets might feel limiting, it presents an opportunity for creativity. A good old-fashioned postage stamp is still a tremendous bargain, and you can fit a lot of affection in one envelope. Recipes, jokes, and drawings add personal touches to your letters without adding to the expense.

In addition to your own concerns about money, children themselves are likely to request money or gifts because they sometimes imagine adults have an endless supply of both. Even teenagers who have a better grasp of finances may challenge you with requests you cannot meet. Just remember that money talks, but it doesn't say much. The effects of your love and attention will last far longer than a video game.

HOW TO USE THIS BOOK

The 40 activities in this book are not a strict set of instructions for a long-distance relationship, but they are divided into three sections to make the ideas as approachable as possible. The first section is about reaching out and getting the ball rolling. The second section offers ways to spend your time when you get together with a young person. The final section includes a variety of approaches for deepening or sustaining your relationship as you get to know each other better over time. Each section is followed by a segment called "Don't Stop Now!" which features additional ideas for moving forward.

You need not read this book in a certain order. If you enjoy cooking, look for the ideas about baking and sending recipes. If your young friend loves to read and write, keep an eye out for suggestions about journaling, reading, and blogging. Pursue the topics that seem most promising to you, and feel free to pick and choose from all of the sections in whatever way you find helpful.

After each idea you'll find a short tip. This may be a reference to another book or a Web site, or it may be a simple piece of advice. Each idea is a starting point rather than a rigid set of directions. Use the tips to help you adapt the suggestions and make them work for your own situation.

BEGIN AT THE VERY BEGINNING

Before you are ready to *maintain* a positive relationship with a young person, you may feel you need to *start* a relationship. Maybe your sister lives in Europe, and you've only met her 7-year-old daughter once. Perhaps you are a dad who went through a really difficult divorce, and you haven't communicated with your ex-wife since. Rest assured that taking time to work through these difficulties will not only bring you closer to the young person you care about, but will also give her or him the positive adult support that is so important to growing up happy and healthy.

Before you attempt to build a bond with a young person you don't know very well, it's a good idea to have a frank discussion with the child's primary parent or caregiver. State your intentions openly and considerately. Tell your married son you'd like to be a loving grandmother to his stepchildren. Explain to your best friend that you aren't planning to have kids of your own, and you'd love to get to know his kids better. Most caregivers will welcome the extra support for their children.

You need to make a similar effort toward the child or teenager. Some kids are immediately thrilled to receive the attention, others are a little more jaded, and some are just shy or unsure how to respond. Whatever the case, it's best to be straightforward and sincere about your interest. Say something simple, such as, "I think you're a great kid, and I was just telling your mom I'd like to know more about you." Don't be discouraged if your comment is met with suspicion or apparent disinterest. Research shows that kids really do need and want caring adults in their lives, no matter how they may act (Scales and Leffert, 2004).

Once you've introduced the idea of being more involved, you can try out the other suggestions in this book as you move forward.

BUT WHAT DO *I* HAVE TO OFFER?

If you are taking the time to read this book and make an effort, you already care about a young person. You want the best for this person, but how much of an impact can you really have from a distance? As it turns out, one caring person *can* make a significant difference in the life of a child.

I work at Search Institute, a nonprofit organization that has been conducting research about children and youth for 46 years. Our surveys and research show compelling evidence that young people thrive through positive relationships with multiple caring adults. We have found that these healthy interactions yield experiences, skills, and strengths that help young people grow into caring, responsible adults. Think of this framework as an adaptable recipe for success. We have identified 40 "ingredients" in this healthy recipe, and we call them Developmental Assets™. See page 119 for a complete list of these assets.

Unfortunately, most young people we surveyed don't experience a majority of the assets. We have surveyed more than 200,000 young people (in grades 6–12) across North America. On average, they report having only 19 assets, and fewer than half of the young people surveyed report receiving support from three or more nonparental adults. No young person can build all of these assets alone, and one or two parents or caregivers cannot simply hand them over. Every young person needs a web of support to build a rich and healthy life.

So what does all of this mean? It means that *you* may be just what a young person needs in her or his life, no matter how close or far away you live from one another. It's not just your hugs, your money, or your physical presence, but your heartfelt support that counts. And this book offers dozens of ideas for showing it.

WHY CARE ABOUT ASSETS?

The Developmental Assets are more than just a research framework; when you take a look at the list, you'll find that they also represent common sense. It seems obvious that young people need positive environments, supportive adults and peers, and enriching experiences in their lives. It is no surprise that these strengths yield powerful results.

Young people who report having few assets are more likely to abuse alcohol, tobacco, and other drugs. Research has found these trends to be true across different racial and ethnic backgrounds, with both genders, in different communities, and in various socioeconomic settings. Low levels of assets are also linked to other high-risk behaviors, including problems in school, violence, antisocial behavior, gambling, eating disorders, and depression (Benson, Roehlkepartain, and Scsma, 2004).

The good news is that young people who report having a greater number of assets are *less* likely to be involved in these negative behaviors. When young people experience more assets, they are consistently more likely to succeed in school, be leaders, value diversity, resist danger, and maintain good health.

You don't have to build all 40 assets in a young person by yourself. Maybe you'll be the person who nurtures a love of reading for pleasure. Maybe you'll enhance a child's cultural competence by sharing information about your home in a different community. Maybe you will be a role model who inspires a young person to have high expectations. You can't single-handedly control all of a child's experiences from a distance, but your unique contribution has the power to help set a young person on a productive course.

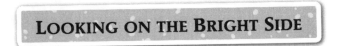

LOOKING ON THE BRIGHT SIDE

You might be thinking, "Sure, assets sound great, but what effect can I have from 300 miles away? It's just too hard!"

It is easy to list the many challenges of a long-distance relationship, but try to focus on the advantages. For example, Virginia teenager Patrick Donlay points out that because he does not see his father (who lives in Minnesota) every day, the two of them don't have fights over life's day-to-day details. If you don't have to argue over rules about curfews and housework, you are already set up for a more harmonious relationship. Similarly, your visits once or twice a year with a young person may coincide with fun holidays or beautiful midsummer weather. You may talk on the phone infrequently, but it can be nice to have several weeks' worth of conversation topics.

Don't forget the added benefit of connecting a young person to the world outside of her or his everyday realm. Whether you live 50 or 5,000 miles away, you offer wisdom and experience from another life, another community—and perhaps another part of the world! Simply seeing through the eyes of a caring "outsider" may open up possibilities that a young person never considered before.

STILL NOT SURE?

You probably agree that being supportive to a young person is important, no matter how far away you live. Perhaps you have some reservations, though. What if your efforts are rejected? How do you keep in touch without e-mail or cell phones? The "Frequently Asked Questions" section (see pages 110–118) at the end of this book addresses these concerns and many others. Feel free to skip ahead to that section now if you're still feeling nervous about getting started, or consult it later as needed.

You might encounter bumps in the road as you proceed. All children and young people may act grouchy, reluctant, suspicious, or downright hostile at times. They can also be brilliant, warm, hilarious, brave, disarming, generous, thought-provoking, trusting, and completely endearing. When you realize how much young people can benefit from your involvement, through the opportunities for creativity, warm support, and positive role modeling that *you* provide, you'll understand that long-distance relationships are truly worth the effort.

ON YOUR WAY

A long-distance relationship can be hard work. It isn't as simple as greeting your teenage neighbor every morning, and it isn't as immediately gratifying as hugging the niece you baby-sit occasionally. When you commit to caring for any young person, though, take heart in knowing that your words and actions can shape their world in ways you don't even realize. While growing up, I rarely saw my Aunt Beth who lives in Alaska, but she sent me some fun and amazing books I might never have read otherwise. I'm sure she had no idea at the time that my love of reading would lead to a career as an editor and a writer.

I hope you'll find, as I have, that young people aren't the only ones to benefit from your efforts. Over time, you may discover that *you* have gained something valuable: a fellow baseball fan, a personal artist for your office wall, or the best friend you always wanted when you were in junior high school. Unexpected joy, humor, and love are some of the incredible rewards of reaching out to a young person no matter how far apart you are.

This book is a tour guide that can accompany you as you

navigate the distance, literally and figuratively. Whether you are just getting started or are simply looking for some fresh ideas, these pages contain experience, strategies, and encouragement to ease your journey. So what are you waiting for? Off you go!

References

Scales, P. C., & Leffert, N. (2004). *Developmental assets: A synthesis of the scientific research on adolescent development*. Minneapolis: Search Institute, p. 27.

Benson, P. L., Rochlkepartain, E. C., & Sesma, A., Jr. (2004). Tapping the power of community: The potential of asset building to strengthen substance abuse prevention efforts. *Search Institute Insights & Evidence 2* (1).

A Knock
at the Door

Whether you are just making your first effort at a long-distance relationship or are attempting to strengthen an existing bond between you and a young person, it can be difficult to decide *how* to reach out. Building a close friendship with someone is tricky even when you see each other all the time; growing closer across geographic distance introduces additional challenges.

The key to getting the ball rolling is to make an effort that is out of the ordinary. A unique or concentrated approach will get the young person's attention and show how interested you truly are. You don't have to spend a lot of time and money to demonstrate this commitment; just paying attention and making a thoughtful gesture is enough.

If you like the idea of growing close to a young person but aren't sure where to begin, this section will offer you a variety of creative options that allow you to reach out even when you don't spend time together in person.

Learn Their Latest Loves

It's a birthday nightmare: You've just spent four weeks scouring the earth for the most popular, thrilling, *perfect* Nintendo® game, only to discover that your nephew has a PlayStation® system. Although age 10 seems a few years shy of adulthood, he explains to you that he hasn't had a Nintendo® system "since I was a kid."

Kids' bodies and minds change at a stunning rate, and so do their tastes. Their opinions about everything from friends to fashion may leave you feeling a bit lost. It might seem easier to avoid all of this hassle and resort to gift certificates or cold hard cash. Don't be discouraged, though. Learning what's "cool" to your stepdaughter can be easy when you take an intentional interest in her likes and dislikes.

Emily O'Connor lives in Colorado, and it is important to her to stay close to her friend's children in the state of Washington. She makes a point of keeping up with their current interests by asking lots of questions when she talks to the kids and their parents. If she knows that her friend's son has recently become a dinosaur fanatic, she'll try to find a toy or an article of clothing with a prehistoric theme.

Paying attention to a young person's preferences isn't just about winning the favorite gift contest, though. Think back to what really mattered to you as a young child, or in high school. Did you have a favorite stuffed animal? Were you obsessed with a celebrity? What did it feel like when you fought with a friend or asked someone on a date? These daily likes and dislikes, trials and triumphs, are the details that mean *everything* to a young person.

So take some time to investigate. Why *is* your granddaughter so crazy about Bratz™ dolls? Who are your son's three best friends? What makes your niece like Thai food, but not Chinese food? You don't need to interrogate them with a long list of rapid-fire inquiries, but show interest by asking a few well-placed follow-up questions. I know from personal experience that it can be difficult to nod and smile during a lengthy description of the musical history of the Foo Fighters, or to remember that your best friend's daughter Arica spells her name "like Africa without the F." But I've also seen how flattered and pleased a kid can be when you remember unique interests and preferences.

You may be mystified—even offended—by the people and hobbies kids like best, but taking the time to discuss what especially matters to them will show how much you care, and help you understand what's meaningful to the young person at that point in time.

· · · · ·

If you want to feel more in the loop when it comes to "kid culture," look for opportunities to learn what's popular. Talk to your neighbors or the teens working in stores, read a children's magazine while you spend time in a waiting room, or browse through the children's and teens' sections of advertising circulars in your Sunday paper.

Millions of Messages

When you send a gift to a young person, fill it with several brief messages or inspiring quotations. For example, you can hide notes in the pages of a book, in the pockets of a jacket, or under each chocolate in a box of mixed chocolates.

Be creative with your messages:

- Use sticky notes to point out your favorite illustrations in a comic book.

- Wrap a gift in plain paper and write jokes all over it. (Don't forget the punch lines!)

- Give a blank journal, but scatter your own encouraging comments, short poems, or photos of yourself as a young person throughout the pages.

- Write personal liner notes to accompany a CD. If you make a mixed CD yourself, add a note about why you chose each song.

- If you send a gift of clothing, use loose stitches to sew your notes all over the outfit.

- Blow up a balloon and write a message on it in permanent marker. Once the ink dries, deflate the balloon and send.

There's no need to stop at these ideas. Come up with your own fun ways to add personal touches to any gift.

Your messages don't have to be profound or wildly hilarious, and your gifts don't have to be costly. The time and effort you put into such a package will demonstrate your exceptional commitment and caring.

• • • • •

Check out www.lotsofjokes.com/kids.htm or yahooligans.yahoo.com/content/jokes for jokes that are appropriate for kids.

Play Games Online

One of the great advantages to modern technology is that it allows people to be "together" even if they're miles apart. Online gaming is a great example of this. Play dominoes with a grandson in Toronto! Challenge your daughter in Mexico City to a game of checkers! As long as you both have access to the Internet, the distance is not an obstacle.

You may be more comfortable if you practice in advance by playing a classic game by yourself. Choose a familiar favorite, such as chess, cribbage, mah-jongg, or Scrabble®. MSN Games and Yahoo! Games have a wide selection of free games, and they answer "Frequently Asked Questions" that are helpful for a new player. If you feel particularly nervous about approaching this activity, try asking a local tech-savvy teenager for advice.

When you are ready to invite a young person to join you, schedule a specific time and "place." You can usually start a virtual game room or enter an existing room. Your invitation may sound like a secret code: "Meet me in the Green Grotto at 9:12." By this time, you will have chosen login names to identify yourselves, and you'll use these names to find each other and play at the same table.

Most game sites allow you to chat with each other using instant messaging, and some even allow you to talk out loud if you have a microphone attached to your computer. Be sure to bring beverages to toast across the wires!

If you and your young friend do not have access to computers and the Internet, take heart. It is possible to adapt some games and play by mail. For example, print out the letters from a game of Boggle or Scrabble®, and see who can come up with the most words. Or use graph paper to play chess, making one move apiece every week. Even simple crossword puzzles or hangman games can be fun for a kid, and you don't have to be in an immediate, heated competition. Simply spending the time "together" is enough of a win.

● ● ● ● ●

To get started playing online games, visit www.zone. msn.com or games.yahoo.com. Many games are only open to teenagers and adults. You can check the suggested age limits for numerous video and computer games at www.mediafamily.org, the Web site for the National Institute on Media and the Family. Don't forget to set a time limit before you begin playing online, as games can often go on indefinitely without prior guidelines.

Lunch Box Love

Mary Ackerman, Search Institute's Director of External Relations, is committed to staying close to her grandchildren. When she wants to send an extra personal touch, she mails tokens their parents can pack in lunch boxes.

Lots of fun items can fit in a lunch box if you use your imagination. Try one of these possibilities:

- Granola bars with notes taped around them;

- Scented stickers with images of food on them;

- A picture of yourself eating lunch with notes about your favorite foods;

- Special napkins with holiday images or favorite cartoon characters;

- Breath mints or dental floss to be used after lunch;

- Homemade fortune cookies; or

- Pages from a 365-day desk calendar. The calendar could be food-related or include daily jokes, cartoons, or vocabulary words.

If you know a young person who doesn't bring boxed lunch to school or who seems to have outgrown this type of treat, try something different. For example, you could send a special wallet or small purse just for carrying lunch money. If a teenager is allowed to leave school grounds for lunch, send a gift certificate for her or his favorite lunch spot.

This type of special gesture shows that even if you are at your office 1,000 miles away, you took the time to brighten a young person's day. It may not be as satisfying as a lunch date in person, but it gives you a chance to stay present on an everyday basis.

• • • • •

Another option is to send a new lunch box at the beginning of each school year. Kids' tastes may change dramatically from year to year, so it is a good idea to check in and find out what they would prefer before investing in a new one.

Get Well Package

The National Long Distance Relationship Building Institute suggests this great idea for long-distance moms, dads, and grandparents: At the beginning of cold and flu season, prepare a care package that contains everything your young friend will need if he or she gets sick. Attach a fun note; for example, "Open this emergency comfort kit when sickness attacks."

As you choose the contents of your kit, consider traditional cold remedies as well as fun items to make the time fly. Here are a few possibilities:

- Packaged or canned chicken soup (of course!); there are also meatless versions of this classic dish for vegetarians;

- Tissues;

- Throat lozenges (make sure to check first for any flavor preferences);

- Saltines or other mild snack foods;

- Juice boxes or bottles of clear, caffeine-free soda;

- Videos or DVDs of favorite movies;

- A special glass for water and other fluids;

- A stuffed animal;

- Age-appropriate novels, comics, picture books, joke books, or puzzle books; or

- A small bell for ringing for help from the couch or bed.

Of course you'll want to send along a personal message with your care package. In addition to your empathy, offer a story about the time that you felt the sickest as a child, or tell about the best doctor or nurse who ever cared for you.

Sympathy and laughter can work wonders. When you can't be there with hugs and jokes, your package of love will deliver plenty of comfort to a kid convalescing on the couch!

• • • • •

For additional activities or information about The National Long Distance Relationship Building Institute, visit www.fambooks.com.

Creative Cards

A standard greeting card is still a lovely way to show you care, but you needn't be limited by the selection at the local drugstore. Try one of these variations for something new:

- **Send an e-card**—Several Web sites offer free e-cards, and many of them include fun music and animations. You can customize these to give them a more personal feel. Try www.freevibe.com for e-cards advocating a drug-free lifestyle, www.moma.org for artistic e-cards from the Museum of Modern Art, or www.hallmark.com for a variety of different e-cards.

- **Send a "found" card**—If you spot something interesting, such as a coupon, brochure, leftover wrapping paper, or shopping bag, use it to make a homemade card.

- **Send a photo card**—Especially near the holidays in December, you can find empty cards that serve as frames for photos. Purchase several in a generic style and choose a photo to send for every occasion.

- **Send a fabric card**—If you enjoy crafts, use fabric paint to spell out your message on a piece of fabric folded like a card. If you are really ambitious or have a high-tech sewing machine, you can even embroider the words!

If you don't think you're a very "crafty" or creative person, there are other ways to make your cards special. For example, my Aunt Ruby has adopted a signature holiday: She has appointed herself the official Easter Bunny in our family. Lots of people send birthday cards or Valentine wishes, but Ruby is one of the only people I know who sends *everybody* a greeting on this occasion.

Kids love to get mail, and the thrill of finding a card in the mailbox is something that few people outgrow. Adding your own flair will make the gesture even more memorable.

• • • • •

Some Web sites will sell your information to advertisers, so be careful where you select your e-cards. For found cards, try asking coworkers for any old office supplies they'd be willing to donate. Outdated letterhead and colorful paperclips can add unique touches to a card.

Send an Instant Picnic

A picnic is already portable by design, so why not send one in the mail? Whether a kid lives near an urban playground, a rural lakeshore, or a national park, an outdoor meal is always a treat. Use this list to plan your package:

- Some processed meats and cheeses are packed so that they do not have to be refrigerated. Peanut butter and jelly are also classic picnic fare. If you pack the bread in a sturdy box or plastic container (to avoid squishing it in transit), they'll have all the fixings for sandwiches.

- Ask for a few extra condiment packets (ketchup, mustard, mayonnaise, etc.) when you go out to eat. If you explain that you're sending them as part of a gift, most restaurants will gladly contribute.

- Packaged goods, such as pudding or fruit cups, dried fruit, crackers, trail mix, and granola bars all travel well by mail.

- Include a variety of juice boxes. The boxes are an easier shape to pack and mail than water bottles or soda cans.

- Send sunglasses, sunscreen, and insect repellent as needed. Be sure to read labels to find products that are safe and age appropriate, and package these items carefully to keep them away from any food items.

- A checkered tablecloth and napkins will add festivity to the event. Add plastic ants for extra silliness!

Once you've packed the basic provisions, don't forget to add some entertainment. Young children may enjoy a butterfly net, sidewalk chalk, or a story, such as *Spot's First Picnic and Other Stories* by Eric Hill (Grosset & Dunlap, 2001). Older kids might like a portable radio, sparklers, a sketchbook, or instructions for a game such as Capture the Flag. A responsible teenager may be ready to use outdoor tools such as a pocketknife or hiking equipment.

Remember that a picnic can be spontaneous and simple, and there are ways to make this idea inexpensive. Lighter foods (potato chips or dried fruit instead of densely packed crackers or nuts) will cut down on the cost of postage. Frisbees®, kites, and soccer balls are often lighter and less costly than other kinds of outdoor equipment. A handwritten letter allows you to send personal wishes and suggestions for activities without spending a fortune on outdoor toys or gadgets. Don't forget to write any extra instructions for younger children who require adult assistance setting up their picnic.

When you've assembled the right mix of food and fun, ship it off to your young picnicker. Be sure to include a self-addressed and stamped postcard for a report on how it went!

■　■　■　■　■

If you are short on time and can afford the convenience, check with specialty stores, grocery stores, or shops at nearby orchards and farms. Many places sell and ship ready-made baskets or picnic boxes.

Photo Diary Exchange

Sending photographs may seem like an obvious way to keep in touch, but many families only send out annual studio portraits or holiday pictures. These charming images are a nice treat, but often reveal very little about the personalities of the kids featured.

If you really want to get a glimpse of life through the eyes of a young person, suggest that he or she keep a photo diary over the course of a day or a week. Send a disposable camera, and request pictures of her or his home, neighborhood, school, and friends. If possible, send money or a coupon for photo processing to have the pictures developed, and ask your young friend to supply captions on the back of each photo to describe the details of daily life.

If you like, you can declare a special theme for the project. Ask the young photographer to take as many pictures as possible of people laughing, or a series of photos showing all of the places where he or she likes to hang out.

Keep a second camera to capture a photo diary of your own. Take pictures of your office, your neighbors, your mode of transportation—anything that shows what your life is like. For kids with a sense of humor, you can write captions, such as "This is the pile of laundry I'm supposed to wash" or "Here is my dog begging to be walked."

If you have access to newer forms of technology, there are all kinds of ways to exchange photos. Use e-mail, camera phones, and Webcams to share instant images. If you have a personal Web site, you can use this as a place to post and exchange photos. As the young person becomes more familiar with you, you'll seem less distant.

• • • • •

Younger children may enjoy the book Flat Stanley *by Jeff Brown (HarperCollins, 2003). Stanley is a boy who is so flat he fits in an envelope, and his parents mail him from place to place. When you send the camera, enclose a paper replica of Stanley, and ask the child to take pictures of Stanley in his new surroundings. You can use this same idea with teenagers, with some minor modifications. Instead of a paper cutout, try making a figurine that resembles the teenager out of molding clay, or attaching a funny picture of her or his face to a pipe-cleaner body.*

Start a Snack Jar

I received my own snack jar from Grandma and Grandpa Gemelke while I was living only three blocks away. If I remember right, I had complained that the rest of my family ate all of the leftover candy bars after Halloween. (I was in middle school, so I didn't have my own trick-or-treat stash.) My grandparents gave me a large ceramic jar shaped like a cartoon cat. Inside I found a variety of candy and snack foods. "You keep this in your bedroom," Grandma said, "and we'll keep it stocked so that you'll always have a little something."

The Gemelke family delights in feeding people, and my grandparents made good on their promise. The snack jar followed me to college, and my grandparents frequently restocked its contents during my trips home. When Grandpa offered me candy from the top shelf of the cupboard, he'd often wink and toss me several extra pieces "for the jar." Grandma even sent me treats by mail to be sure that my sweet tooth was always satisfied.

Those sugary gifts were great, of course, but the jar itself is what made this such a special memory. Kids are often at the mercy of adults when it comes to food, and it was so nice to have a secret stash that was *mine*. When I was transitioning into adulthood during college, it was also comforting to enjoy treats that came from loved ones instead of the cafeteria or the snack shop.

If you'd like to start a snack jar for a young person, you need not purchase anything fancy. Use dish soap and baking soda to wash out an empty tomato sauce or mayonnaise jar, and decorate the outside with permanent markers, construction paper, paint, or stickers. When you want to give healthier snacks, choose energy bars, nut clusters, or small boxes of raisins or dried fruit instead of candy. Be sure to give only individually wrapped items to avoid attracting ants and other pests.

· · · · ·

Consider decorating or sending a new jar each year. You can choose something that reflects the young person's changing tastes. Don't forget to check in with parents or guardians before sending any food; some children have food allergies, and others aren't allowed to eat sugary snacks.

Instruct via Video

If you have access to a video camera, you can send your face and your voice anywhere in the world. Young people who only hear your voice on the phone might love the chance to see your face on screen. Many people are camera-shy, though, and don't know what to say once the tape is rolling. If you are one of these people, consider using video to demonstrate one of your hobbies or a common task.

When you are good at something, doing it makes you feel comfortable and confident. This can alleviate some of the anxiety of being on camera. Think about the possibilities, and tape an instructional video to introduce a young person to your talent or interest. Here are a few examples:

- Did you know many teenage boys are becoming interested in knitting? According to www.MenKnit. net, there are thousands of men and boys around the world who enjoy knitting. You could give one lesson in person during a visit and tape additional lessons for later viewing.

- If you know a teenager who recently obtained a driver's license, make a video showing how to change a flat tire. This is a tool he or she can refer to long after Driver's Ed is over.

- Invite a young person to send you interview questions, then respond to them on videotape. If you're feeling creative, you can even create your own talk show format, like "Gabbin' with Grandpa" or "Aunt Lisa's Variety Show." When you mail the tape, be sure to send your own interview questions to learn more about your young friend.

- Even the most basic tasks can fascinate young children. (Watch *Mr. Rogers' Neighborhood* or *Baby Einstein* if you don't believe me!) Talk to the video camera while you dust your knickknacks or arrange photos in an album.

- Do you enjoy fitness activities, like yoga or modern dance? You don't have to be Richard Simmons to shake your buns on camera!

- I once videotaped myself cleaning and filleting fish to show my dad I could do it. He loved it! Mundane tasks like these can seem interesting on tape. If you choose this option, invite the young person to send you a tape demonstrating her or his own skills.

If you're having trouble thinking of an idea, check out the how-to videos at your public library. These might help you identify which of your skills will lend themselves to an instructional recording.

Videos will turn out best when you have plenty of light and someone else running the camera. Production quality isn't really the point, though. This is a chance for you to have fun and to show your young friend a new side of yourself.

• • • • •

You may be able to borrow video equipment through a local cable access station. If you are willing to show your video on the air, you may be able to use the camera at no charge.

Distant Delivery

One convenient technological advance is the ability to use credit cards nearly everywhere. You may already have discovered that you can order pizza this way over the phone—but why not order pizza halfway across the country?

This pleasant surprise requires a bit of advance detective work. Start with a phone call to the young person's parent or guardian to choose a convenient mealtime and to write down favorite pizza toppings. You can ask the adult for the phone number of a local pizza place, or you can search through a telephone directory on the Internet or in a book. You might discover that the restaurant you've chosen allows online ordering, like Pizza Hut or Papa John's. If not, call the pizzeria in advance to make sure it's okay to place an order from a remote location. Some places require photo identification upon delivery of the pizza, so you may need to explain the situation.

Once the details are in place, make the final arrangements for a surprise dinner delivery. If you like, you can plan it to follow a hard exam or important sports competition.

Ask the pizza delivery person or the young person's caregiver to share a brief greeting from you when the pizza arrives.

If pizza isn't a favorite, investigate other options. Some cities have a wide variety of restaurants, bakeries, and candy shops that will deliver anything from chow mein to freshly baked cookies. Although small towns have fewer eating establishments, you may be able to connect with a kind manager who will help you send a special treat.

• • • • •

For another option, consider sending a gift certificate or a gift card to a kid-friendly restaurant. Even a few dollars at a fast-food restaurant may feel like a luxury to someone who doesn't go out for dinner often.

Be an Old-Fashioned Pen Pal

When her best friend's son, Willie, left for college, Karen Bartig spotted an opportunity to be a positive influence in his life. Karen was well aware of how valuable a supportive adult could be to a young person and she wanted to make sure that no matter how great the distance between them, Willie would still know how much she cared.

Willie is a good writer who loves to correspond with family and friends. Karen keeps in touch with him throughout the school year, and he always writes back. She writes about her daily life, sends postcards, and shares booklets and brochures from the various events she attends and places she visits. She is always looking for an unusual card to make each letter more interesting. She, in turn, enjoys learning about his life at college.

Writing a simple letter may seem like a no-brainer, but consistent correspondence is a surprisingly powerful force. Karen notes that she and Willie now keep up with each other in a way they never did when he lived nearby.

You may take your own unique approach to this idea.

Perhaps you can start a postcard tradition. Whether you travel around the world or simply stop at a gas station in a neighboring state or province, you can keep your eyes open for new postcards to send to your young friend.

If writing is not your style, use audio recordings to send messages back and forth. When Ruth Taswell was in grade 7, her older sister was a foreign exchange student. Instead of sending handwritten notes, they mailed recorded "letters." A cassette is not quite as easy to mail as a letter, but it adds the immediacy of a friendly voice.

Try to view letter writing not as a quaint, old-fashioned mode of communication, but as a timeless strategy for staying in touch. E-mail may be the way some young people prefer to send messages, but rest assured that "snail mail" messages will never go out of style.

• • • • •

You can find some great deals on stationery after Valentine's Day and when school supplies go on sale in the fall. Take advantage of opportunities like these to stock up inexpensively for the whole year. Discount stores, thrift stores, and garage sales can also be excellent sources for inexpensive paper and pens.

Baking from Afar

Nothing beats my dad's butter-pecan cookies or my grandma's fresh bread. Care packages are always wonderful surprises, of course, but perhaps you know an older child who is ready to brave the kitchen himself, or a teenager with a budding reputation as "the family chef." Instead of sending prepared goodies, consider sending the ingredients and the recipe for his favorite snack.

It is important to gauge a child's abilities in food preparation to avoid kitchen catastrophes. Enlist the help of a parent or another adult who lives with your young friend when you decide what to send. Your 16-year-old daughter may be ready to make your famous pumpkin cheesecake, but try one of these simpler ideas for a novice:

- **Caramel apples**—Apples, caramels, sticks, and waxed paper are all you need for this carnival favorite.

- **Crispy rice treats**—This microwaveable recipe calls for only three ingredients: marshmallows, butter or margarine, and crispy rice cereal.

- **Trail mix**—Just send a variety of raw materials, such as peanuts, raisins, pretzels, almonds, chocolate chips, dates, dried cranberries, crunchy cereal, or sunflower seeds. Even a young child can mix favorites for the perfect combination.

In addition to the ingredients, be sure to send instructions and a list of the utensils, bowls, and other necessary equipment. If the recipe calls for something out of the ordinary, such as a pastry cutter, you may want to include that item as part of your package. Older teenagers might be ready to think about food presentation, or to tackle a meal with more than one course. Consider sending them tips on appropriate serving dishes and ideas for pairing different dishes together by flavor or ethnicity.

If the child has access to a speakerphone, you can arrange a time to call on the telephone and make the goodies together. If not, be sure to check in later to ask how the culinary adventure turned out.

• • • • •

The first recipes I prepared as a child came from the New Junior Cook Book *from Better Homes and Gardens. If you are looking for recipes to send, check out the latest version of this classic.*

Audio/Visual Scavenger Hunt

Kids of all ages love scavenger hunts, and this activity is even more fun if you encourage them to invite friends or siblings to join them.

Find out if the young person has access to a video camera, a still camera, or a tape recorder. A disposable camera will do just fine, so you can send one in the mail if you like. As you generate the list of hunted items, tailor them to the equipment the young person will be using. Here are some examples:

- **Video items**—a person waving, a stoplight changing color, a dog rolling over, or a toddler walking.

- **Still camera items**—a spider, a street sign, a recycling bin, a teacher, or a briefcase.

- **Audio items**—someone singing a popular song, a car horn honking, birds singing, a phone ringing, or a person playing the guitar or harmonica.

It is also possible to do an Internet scavenger hunt, but I don't recommend trying this without an adult to supervise the search. It is too easy for a young person to stumble across pornography, commercial scams, or simply inaccurate information.

Over the telephone or in your written instructions, be sure to cover some ground rules. Remind the young person not to approach strangers alone, and to ask permission before recording or photographing people or personal property. Make a plan for the hunter to submit the found items on an audio recording, on videotape, on film, or as digital photos attached to an e-mail. Set a goal (e.g., 12 of the 15 items listed), and schedule a deadline a week or two later.

Scavenger hunts can be hard work, so try to build in a reward. Announce that you'll send a book, a gift card, or a CD if the young person captures at least half of the items. Even a congratulatory card afterward will make the effort seem more fun. You could also offer to take her or him out for a special meal the next time you're together. And don't forget to invite the young person to send *you* on a scavenger hunt, too.

■ ■ ■ ■ ■

Public libraries often have books about planning children's parties, and scavenger hunts frequently appear in them. You can adapt the scavenger hunt lists from party books for this activity. The inspiration for this idea came from Generators, *a book of intergenerational activities (Search Institute, 2005).*

Don't Stop Now!

Here are some additional ideas for getting a long-distance relationship off the ground:

- Find out what the young person is studying in school and send a themed "field trip in a box" for the whole class. For example, if the class is studying plants, you could send samples of the ones that are native to your region, or mail appropriate treats like sunflower seeds.

- Write stories together. Take turns writing what happens next, one sentence or paragraph at a time. If you use mail, send a self-addressed, stamped envelope to make it easier for the young person to respond. You might also write in comic-book style or use this same method to write a song together.

- Send a different piece of weather-related sports equipment on the first day of each season. For example, send swimming gear to a warm climate on the first day of summer, or send ice skates to a cold climate on the first day of winter.

- Ask a young person for advice with a problem. Talk about a friend who has hurt your feelings or a task that you're having trouble completing. This shows that you value her or his opinion, and you may really benefit from a new perspective.

Now That We're Together

When you *do* have a chance to spend time with a young person, you may feel nervous about making the most of your time together. What kinds of things will you do? What on earth will you talk about? How will you make the limited time meaningful and memorable?

The ideas in this section address the complications of planning time with a young person who lives apart from you. Whether you see each other once a month or once a year, sporadic visits make it difficult to maintain closeness. Here you'll find strategies, activities, and rituals that foster commitment and continuity.

Get There When You Can

A divorced man in Chicago had plans to attend his son's baseball playoffs in Centreville, Virginia. As the first game approached, the father was diagnosed with Bell's palsy, a temporary nerve condition that affects the muscles of the face. As part of his treatment, his doctor insisted that he avoid flying in an airplane.

The father knew his son would be upset. When they spoke on the phone, he was careful to describe the condition in a way that would not frighten his son. Then he prepared to drop the real bomb. When he explained that he was unable to fly, he asked his son, "Do you know what this means for your baseball game?"

The son paused for a moment before he answered. Then, with the questioning tone of someone deciphering a math problem, he replied, "You're driving?" When this stunned father considered what his son said, he surprised himself by answering, "Yes, that's exactly right. I'm driving!"

It breaks your heart when you have to say no to a child. You probably do not have endless quantities of time and money. Your job schedule may be inflexible, or you may have other family commitments that make it difficult to travel. But before you decide these obstacles are insurmountable, take some time to think about what it means when you say "I can't." Some people truly can't come up with the finances to travel long distances, and maybe that's your situation. Other times, "I can't" means "That's very difficult" or "I have different priorities right now." These are legitimate reasons to delay a trip. But when you *can* get there, your presence is one of the greatest gifts you can give.

The next time your loved one has a big piano recital or a birthday party, see if you can make it there. Your attendance will show your feelings in a way nothing else can.

· · · · ·

You may have already discovered that Web sites like www.priceline.com, www.travelocity.com, www. orbitz.com, and www.expedia.com are great resources for inexpensive travel options. You can also contact AAA or CAA for discounts and free maps kids can use to track your trip. Check with Amtrak (www.amtrak. com), Via Rail (www.viurail.ca), and Greyhound (www.greyhound.com) for train and bus trips.

Ask an Unexpected Question

When you find yourself at a family gathering, struggling to make small talk with relatives you haven't seen in months or even years, a conversation with a 13-year-old may seem particularly daunting. Whether that grandson, niece, or younger cousin is smiling nervously around the room or scowling in front of the television, there's a good chance that he or she feels as awkward as you do. This is a great opportunity to reach out, no matter how scary or unwelcome it may feel.

Young people are always answering questions such as "How is school going?" or "Do you have a boyfriend/girl-friend?" These questions are fine for getting started, but are more likely to elicit one-word answers such as "Fine" or "Yeah." To get an engaging response, ask an engaging question! You might try one of the following suggestions:

- Who is your favorite adult in the universe?

- What is the best book you have read or movie you've seen in the last year?

- What do you like about your parents, teachers, or school? What is one thing you wish you could change about them?

- How have popular music and television changed in your lifetime?

- What's the most annoying question an adult has ever asked you?

Don't give up if you strike out with the first question. I once tried to start a conversation with a teenager at a holiday party, and he was extremely reluctant to talk to me about school or his friends. When he said he played in a rock band, I started asking follow-up questions about his guitar playing and his favorite performers. He suddenly brightened and began talking animatedly about the industrial-rock musicians who had influenced him. I didn't know much about the topic, but my willingness to listen was enough to keep the conversation going for 20 minutes.

When you do stumble upon the magic question that sparks a connection, file that information away for later use. As you write letters, purchase gifts, or try some of the ideas in this book, you'll be able to show that you were paying attention to a young person's unique interests.

• • • • •

Check out The Kids' Book of Questions *by Gregory Stock to find some provocative questions to ask young people (Workman Publishing Company, Inc., 2004).*

Scrape Together a Scrapbook

The very word "scrapbook" makes some people cringe with intimidation. They think about the recent trend toward elaborate archives—full of captions, stickers, and die-cut paper shapes. If that sounds daunting to you, the following approach may be more appealing.

When Philip Donlay was a little boy, his grandmother would page through magazines with him. When Philip saw a picture that he liked, they would cut it out and paste it into a simple notebook. Before long they had a book filled with a hodgepodge of images: airplanes, hunting, fishing, dogs, cars. The only thing the images had in common was that Philip chose them.

Philip has held onto this scrapbook over the years. As he pages through it, he is amazed to see his current preferences reflected in this book. He still enjoys hunting and fishing, and he remains interested in dogs and cars. He and his grandmother also clipped advertisements for commercial airlines; today, Philip is a pilot, and has written a suspense novel called *Category Five* about air travel during a hurricane.

During your visit with a young person, keep your eyes peeled for potential scrapbook materials. Clip articles on national or international events from newspapers on those days you are together. Grab a take-out menu or a business card from a favorite restaurant where the two of you eat. Remember that even a candy wrapper may be a source of great nostalgia when the child is an adult.

• • • • •

If you are looking for free magazines, check with your local library at the end of the year. They often discard older magazines when the new year's subscriptions begin. You can also purchase magazines inexpensively at many garage sales and thrift stores.

18

Go for a Drive

When she was a little girl, Joy Hilton treasured her visits to her grandparents' home in Alabama. Although she always enjoyed her grandmother's special pot roast and their traditional ice cream sundaes on Saturday night, Joy especially loved the ritual car rides with her grandfather. They would look at old southern mansions, sing traditional songs, and drive around the nearby mountains.

Going for a drive is a great activity, because it can be adapted for kids of all ages. Younger children might enjoy looking out the window and playing I Spy, and young adults may be thrilled at a chance to use a new learner's permit or driver's license. The privacy of a car is a great place to have a serious chat or loudly sing a favorite song along with the radio. Kids are less likely to feel self-conscious while you've got your eyes on the road, and you may find that they talk more openly than they would on the telephone or at the dinner table.

If you don't have a car, you can make a point of riding the train or bus, or taking a taxi ride together during your visits. You could also borrow or rent bicycles and enjoy a leisurely outing in the neighborhood or at a nearby park. Try choosing destinations that neither of you have visited before, or make it a point to return to the same scenic overlook every year. Remember that even simple pleasures acquire a lasting meaning when you turn them into rituals. As Joy advises, "Take something personal and make it a tradition."

• • • • •

Look into package deals when you book your travel arrangements. You may be able to get a very inexpensive deal on a car rental if you place your reservation at the same time you purchase a plane ticket, for example.

Talk to the Animals

Pets can be an important source of responsibility and friendship for kids. A 5-year-old may have lengthy conversations or imaginary adventures with her guinea pig, and a teenager who is facing social challenges may feel as if his cat is the only creature on the planet that will comfort him without adding to his problems. When you're dealing with a young animal lover, be sure to show some interest and respect toward these nonverbal family members.

Petting animals and talking to them are obvious ways to be supportive. You might also ask to see an animal's tricks or talents, and you can ask permission to offer treats as a reward. If you're feeling more ambitious, help your young friend with responsibilities such as feeding a snake, grooming a horse, or cleaning a lizard's aquarium.

In addition to paying attention to a pet while you are visiting, try some long-distance strategies. You may not want to mark the hamster's birthday in your calendar, but you can always send along a little something when you mail a package for the child's birthday. Some treats, such as catnip or birdseed, will even fit in an envelope. Or your gesture may be something simpler, like remembering to say, "Give your puppy a scratch behind the ears for me."

If kids aren't allowed to have pets due to allergies or family boundaries, you may be able to find other ways to honor a love of animals. Ask a parent or caregiver if it's okay to send a hummingbird feeder for the apartment balcony or a squirrel feeder for the backyard. When you visit young people who can't have their own pets, try spending time with the animals at a local shelter. Teenagers might enjoy going a step further and spending the day volunteering together at an animal shelter.

It's okay if you aren't crazy about animals yourself. In fact, you can use your discomfort to start a conversation: "I'm afraid of mice, and I've seen how comfortable you are with Mr. Cheese. Can you think of anything I could do to make myself feel safer when I'm around rodents?" Simply acknowledging the importance of favorite animals is enough to show that you're paying attention.

· · · · ·

No matter how much a young person loves animals, you should never give an animal as a gift without first consulting with her or his parent or caregiver. Animals are a lot of work, and they deserve loving homes, so it's important to have an adult on board with such a big commitment.

Slang Dictionary

Few experiences make a person feel more thoroughly out of touch than an inability to understand current slang. If you find yourself staring blankly when you offer a treat and your grandson replies, "Fo' shizzle, Grizzle," this may be the perfect activity to bring the two of you closer together.

When you introduce the idea, you might start by talking about the slang you used as a child or teenager. Whether you are from the "Whoa, heavy" generation or the "Gag me with a spoon" generation, the sayings from your youth may be truly amusing to a young person. Once you share some of your own memories, ask about a modern word or phrase that you find confusing. If you learn "That's hot" means "That's cool," you might talk about when you first heard that "bad" meant "good." Pointing out similarities will help you find common ground and make the conversation more entertaining.

Invite your young friend to join you in writing down definitions for words and phrases that have been popular during your lifetimes. You might use a notebook, index cards, or a word-processing program to capture your dictionary entries. Use each of the terms in a sentence to help convey their meaning. You might even include favorite movie quotes or the names of television characters who have made particular expressions popular.

If an older child or teenager seems unenthusiastic about making a dictionary, try tinkering with the format. Sometimes older kids are more interested in participating in this type of project if they imagine it as a training tool for someone younger. If you call the dictionary *The New Kid's Guide to Junior High Slang,* it might feel less like homework and more like an enjoyable activity. Or perhaps your young friend would be more interested in making an audio recording.

However you choose to proceed, it's important to remember that learning slang will *not* make you cool. On the contrary, young people are likely to roll their eyes even more dramatically if they hear you trying to use their words. Imitating the way they sound and making fun of their words can hurt their feelings and undermine your credibility. Keep the focus on *understanding* each other rather than *mimicking* one another.

What's your bag? What's your damage? What's your deal? What's the haps? What's the sitch? Where my dogs at? Your dictionary may not be able to answer *all* of these questions, but it will offer a fun step toward comprehending each other better.

• • • • •

Any discussion of slang introduces the possibility of "naughty" or impolite words. Be as discreet as possible when you define your own phrases. ("Make love, not war," has more than one interpretation, so opt for the nonsexual one.) If your young friend introduces a term that seems inappropriate or offensive to you, try to talk about it and set boundaries before resorting to any disciplinary measures.

Go for the Green

Whether kids are 6 or 16, they can enjoy the call of the wild. Make use of whatever green space is available by inviting your young friend to step outside during your visit. Spend some time at a city park, stroll around the farm, or explore every inch of the backyard. The options can be impressive when you use your imagination.

Inviting a young person outside serves multiple purposes. For one thing, it allows you to get away from the distractions of other people and really pay attention to each other. For kids who spend a lot of time plugged into computers and cell phones, it offers a new focus and a unique experience. For those who love the outdoors, it gives them a chance to be the experts; in this case, you can request detailed commentary from your young tour guide.

Pat Howell-Blackmore of Paris, Ontario, uses nature to reconnect with her childhood friend Meagan and Meagan's children. As girls, Pat and Meagan grew up in St. George, Ontario, a rural area where biking and walking to each others' houses was the norm. When Meagan moved away and began a family, Pat wanted to build a connection with her best friend's two sons. She decided to fly to Meagan's home in Esquimalt, British Columbia, once a year, and on every visit the two women make a point of taking the boys to the nearby Pacific Ocean. Initially, the boys tagged along as infants in strollers, but as they grew older and learned to walk, beachcomb, and rock climb, these trips became opportunities to showcase their new talents to "Auntie Pat," and a chance for Pat and Meagan to relate stories from their own childhoods about mastering these skills.

Remember that not everybody wants to stop and smell the roses. Flowers are one great focus for a nature walk, but maybe your nephew prefers to look for birds' nests or butterfly cocoons. Your daughter may want to examine anthills or spider webs. Perhaps a teen will be more interested in a vegetable garden or identifying different types of trees. You'll have better luck if you spend the time doing something that appeals to both of you rather than setting the agenda yourself.

Walks can also be a chance to help a community. When you're out together on an expedition, kids of any age can take a garbage bag and clean up trash they see along the way. Make this service activity into a tradition by cleaning up the same area during each visit.

Whatever you choose to do, be sure to tell your young friend how much you value the experience. If you feel discouraged by rain or wind or boredom, remind yourself that being together is the most important goal.

• • • • •

When weather is a major obstacle, look for indoor green spaces. You might consider arboretums, greenhouses, and indoor courtyards at offices and hotels. If none of the ideas above are readily available, help a child experience nature by giving her or him a plant, a bulb, or some seeds to grow on a windowsill.

Go Geocaching or Letterboxing

Did you ever wish you could find an old-fashioned treasure map where "X" marks the spot? Geocaching may be the modern answer to this fantasy. Participants use a Global Positioning System (GPS) device to locate a hidden cache, or a container filled with semi-valuable items. People bring an item with them, and when they reach the cache, they take something out of it as a "treasure" and leave something else behind. A cache may contain any variety of plunder: games, videos, money, toys, hiking tools, jewelry, CDs—even maps to other geocaches! Caches often contain logbooks so participants can record their transactions for future visitors to read about.

Plan a geocaching excursion the next time you get together with your young friend. Many geocaches are hidden in remote wilderness areas, but others appear in cities. (A quick Internet search reveals 11 of them to be found within 2 miles of my office in downtown Minneapolis!) Chances are there will be at least one located nearby, and this joint adventure will give the two of you a chance to have fun while working together toward a goal.

Geocaching can be an expensive endeavor to begin; one GPS unit costs approximately $100. However, some electronic organizers and cellular telephones now include this feature, and the increasing popularity of geocaching may result in more affordable equipment on the market.

If geocaching is cost prohibitive, you might try letterboxing instead. Less dependent on exact coordinates, letterboxing relies on a list of clues. The letterbox usually consists of a waterproof container with a logbook and a rubber stamp inside. Instead of taking and leaving objects behind, people bring personal rubber stamps and inkpads to mark their visit in the hidden logbook, and they use the letterbox stamp to mark their personal logbook showing that they have visited the letterbox.

Because geocaching and letterboxing are already long-distance in nature, they are also perfect activities to share across the miles. If you and a young person get excited about this idea, you can report your separate discoveries to each other. If you both visit the same location in a year, you can even plan to leave messages for each other in the logbook.

*　*　*　*　*

For extensive explanations about the process of geocaching, visit www.geocaching.com. For more information about geocaching with kids, visit www.eduscapes.com/ geocaching. If you'd like to explore letterboxing, check out www.letterboxing.org/.

Create an Altered Book

"[An altered book is] any book, old or new, that has been recycled by creative means into a work of art."
—*International Society of Altered Book Artists*

An altered book can be a fantastic vessel for artistic expression, especially for older children and teenagers. It begins with an idea such as drawing a mustache on a book illustration, and there's no telling how far the artist can go.

First, you'll need a "canvas," or a used book that is ripe for altering. Yard sales, thrift stores, library sales, and used book stores are good sources. You want to choose a book that is already visually interesting in some way. Experienced artists can make magic with any book, but you'll probably have better luck with a book that contains plenty of photos or illustrations. For example, you might look for a book of fashion sewing projects from the '60s, a tattered children's picture book, or a guidebook for identifying birds or insects. For added significance, have your young friend choose a book about her or his favorite (or least favorite) school subject, or find a used copy of a book he or she has read recently.

After you've chosen a book, alter some of the pages yourself:

- Cut a hole in the middle of a page to create a window showing the image on the next page.

- Clip celebrity heads out of popular magazines and glue them on the bodies of animals. Add speaking balloons and funny captions to some of the photos in the book.

- Cut words and sentences from a discarded encyclopedia or dictionary and insert them in bizarre locations.

Once you've demonstrated the idea, share the book with your young friend and invite her or him to complete the project with you. This can also be a good long-distance project if you decide to mail the book back and forth to one another, making additional changes each time. Suggest turning the book into something wild or funny or beautiful. If you want to offer further inspiration, bring rubber stamps, scrapped catalogs, markers, and irregular-edged scissors.

This activity can be a little dangerous with a young child who does not yet understand when and why it's okay to alter certain books. Be sure to explain the activity as an art project, and emphasize that you are recycling a book that is no longer in use.

Show plenty of enthusiasm when you see the finished product. Your young friend may feel uncertain about the goal of this activity, so make it clear that creative fun is enough to make it worthwhile. Make a point of noticing unique touches, and ask if you can have the book as a keepsake.

• • • • •

If you'd like to see some elaborate examples or learn more about this hobby, visit www.alteredbookartists. com. The book Altered Art: Techniques for Creating Altered Books, Boxes, Cards & More *by Terry Taylor applies similar ideas to objects beyond books (Sterling Publishing Company, Inc., 2004). You can also try making your own books from scratch; check out* Making Books That Fly, Fold, Wrap, Hide, Pop Up, Twist, and Turn *by Gwen Diehn for ideas and step-by-step instructions (Lark Books, 1998).*

Scent Memory

My husband and I moved from Fargo, North Dakota, to Brooklyn, New York, in January of 2001. It was hard to say goodbye to many friends and family members, but parting with our nieces was the most difficult. They were 3 and 5 years old at the time, and I was sure they would forget all about me and turn into strangers. I could stay in touch with my sister-in-law and other adults by e-mail, but my nieces needed hugs and kisses and stories. I dreaded the effects of the distance.

My fears were put to rest months later when my sister-in-law's friend visited their house. My older niece, Shayna, told the woman, "You smell like my Auntie Tenessa." They figured out that the woman had washed her hair with the same shampoo I use. Shayna and her younger sister, Shelby, had spent hours "fixing" my hair when I lived nearby, so the mere scent of my shampoo was enough to keep me present in their minds.

Scientists have proven that scent is one of the strongest triggers for memory. Use this sensory wonder to record memorable experiences with a young person. When you are together, point out the smell of mowed grass at a park, or bake cookies and talk about the delicious aroma. Consider sharing scented products like shampoo or sunscreen that can remind you both of each other when you're apart. Even calling attention to less pleasant smells, like the indescribable stink of a subway, will give firm roots to the memory of an outing.

Take this notion to the next level by planning an intentional smelling activity. Blindfold your young friend while you make dinner and ask her or him to sniff and guess each ingredient and the final dish. If you like to wear cologne or perfume, invite your young friend to join you in dabbing some on each morning that you're together. Sit together outdoors and have a contest to see who can identify the greatest number of distinct smells.

● ● ● ● ●

Give your letters and packages added dimension by including themed scents. If you're writing about spring weather, include a pressed flower. Insert a small cedar chip to enhance a note about sitting by a roaring fire. In addition, many inexpensive gifts for kids, such as stickers, stationery, and markers, come in a variety of scents. Teenagers might prefer bath salts, cologne, or sachets filled with dried flowers. Try putting a few drops of your cologne or perfume on your letters to add a heightened feeling of closeness.

25

Give Them Space

If you've been gearing up for a visit with a young person, you may have a packed agenda: visiting a local historical site, shopping for clothing, going camping, baking cookies, attending a basketball game, and having a heart-to-heart chat about the importance of a good education. When you love someone you rarely see and you have high hopes for the time you *do* get to spend together, your expectations can become a bit unrealistic.

The reality is that kids have their own interests and will join your activities (or not) at their own pace. Rigid schedules simply don't work with a 4-year-old, and a high-school student may get a little twitchy if she can't check her e-mail for two days.

Teenager Patrick Donlay says that one great thing his dad does is leave time for him to spend with his friends. His father travels halfway across the country to visit him, but assures him that he doesn't want to make Patrick feel as if he's a prisoner. Even if Philip simply hangs out by himself in his hotel room for an evening, he knows how important the time is to his son. This freedom makes the visit much more pleasant for both of them, because Patrick is a willing participant in the rest of their plans.

It's okay to feel disappointed when a child seems disinterested in your suggestions, but try not to play the role of the enforcer. Your limited time together is precious. Let your young friend spend some time alone, and you'll both have fonder memories of the visit.

• • • • •

Before your trip, ask the young person to help you find ways to spend time alone during your visit. He or she can help you identify local museums or stores that may give you something to do while allowing them some free time.

Delayed Discoveries

"I wish you could stay!" Nothing makes you feel more loved than these five words uttered by a child. This sentiment may inspire you to leave a little bit of yourself behind when you are visiting a child.

Before your departure, take some time to hide notes or surprises around the young person's home. Make each little token relevant to the location where you hid it. If possible, leave several signed messages that will be discovered at various times. Here are a few possibilities:

- In a box or bottle of children's medication, leave a note that says, "I'm sorry you're not feeling well."

- Leave a note that says "Sweet Dreams!" on the pillow.

- Insert a personalized CD into a teenager's compact disc player.

- Leave a cartoon in the refrigerator that says, "Don't forget to eat your vegetables!"

- If the young person has a driveway or sidewalk outside of the home, use chalk to draw pictures or write a farewell poem.

- Slip a novelty pen into a backpack or school tote bag.

- Tape a greeting card inside the next page of a calendar.

- With the guardian's permission, use soap or lipstick to write "Looking good!" or "Have a great day!" on the bathroom mirror. You can also leave messages that don't require any clean-up by letting the mirror get steamed over during a hot shower, then "writing" in the condensation with your finger. Let the message dissipate until it's no longer visible. When the mirror gets fogged up during the next shower, the message will reappear.

- Put a note in a young athlete's cleats or duffel bag that says "Good luck at the game" or "Knock one out of the park for me!"

Feel free to be as silly as you like. Since you won't be around when your young friend notices each message, you don't have to worry about feeling embarrassed for saying the wrong thing.

Regardless of what memento you choose to leave behind, you'll make the point that you're still thinking of them even after you've left physically.

• • • • •

This is a good opportunity for you to connect with a young person's parent or caregiver. Enlist their help in concealing the items or ask that they reveal or deliver items gradually in the days after you've left.

A Fond Farewell

Saying goodbye can be sad, but planning a special send-off can make the departure fun and meaningful. Try something new each time, or start a ritual for every parting. Here are a few ideas you might consider:

- Make a trip to an ice cream shop right before you have to leave each other.

- Take a walk and look for two special stones. Each of you can keep one to remind you of the time you spent together.

- Play a favorite board game or video game together one last time. Make plans for a rematch during your next visit.

- Get up early and have breakfast together on the day when one of you is leaving. Head to a favorite restaurant, or have a cereal picnic outside somewhere.

- Hand over a note or a letter to be opened after your visit.

- If you're near a body of water, write or carve a word describing your time together on a piece of driftwood. Throw it into the lake, river, or ocean and watch it drift away together.

Think about your own relationship and personalize these final moments. If the traditional butterfly kisses are met with eye rolling, try a different approach. Young children might like a special hug or kiss, but an older child might prefer a funny handshake. A teenager who is going through a tough time emotionally might respond better to a heartfelt conversation the night before you leave.

Sometimes kids will act distracted or even a little callous when it's time to say goodbye. They may be feeling sad, too, but are unsure how to express it. Remember that no matter how a child acts, your last gesture of sincere interest is a chance for you to leave a loving impression.

■ ■ ■ ■ ■

This idea was inspired by the book Playful Reading: Positive, Fun Ways to Build the Bonds between Preschoolers, Books, and You *by Carolyn Munson-Benson (Search Institute, 2004).*

Don't Stop Now!

Try one of these bonus activity ideas when you and your long-distance friend get together:

- Purchase a season pass to a state or regional park, museum (children's museum, science museum, art museum), sports team, or zoo. Encourage kids to make use of the season pass whether you're together or apart.

- Invite one or two of the young person's close friends along when you spend time together. Simple activities like dinner, a walk, or a pickup game of basketball become even more memorable when you include the peers who are important to your young friend. He or she may also open up a little more around friends than an adult.

- Give your young friend a charm bracelet, and add a new charm each time you see each other.

- Read the newspaper together. Talk about local and national headlines, and ask for the young person's opinions.

- Select a favorite book together and release it "into the wild" (at a park, a doctor's office, a restaurant, etc.) to be discovered and read by a stranger. Visit www.bookcrossing.com to learn how to track the whereabouts of the book.

Don't Be a Stranger

Even if you already have a strong long-distance relationship with a young person, it can be challenging to sustain closeness over time. Children develop new interests as they grow older, and relationships shift and change whether you are together or not. When you spend a lot of time apart from each other, intentional effort is even more crucial to keeping a close friendship alive.

Some suggestions in this section offer new approaches for kids of different ages; some are simply about getting to know each other better. Others focus on repeated traditions that foster a lasting bond. These strategies will help you look for fresh ideas as you continually strive to be a positive influence in the life of a young person.

28

Personalize a Phone Card

A phone card is a great option when you are trying to connect with an older child or a teenager. Children feel important when they have "real cards" to put in their wallets, and free calling gives teens a feeling of independence—especially if you encourage them to use some of the minutes to call their friends. The trick is to get the young person to use the card to call *you*.

It is often a challenge to get a child or a teenager to initiate a conversation. Before sending a calling card, take a few moments to add a personal touch. Here are a few ideas you might try:

- Type a fake newspaper ad for "Aunt Carla's Listening Hotline."

- Make a list of "Top Ten Reasons to Call Your Grandpa."

- Draw a cartoon of yourself waiting by the telephone. Add a message like, "I'm always here to talk" or "Can't wait to hear from you."

- Include an incentive with the calling card. Tell a younger child that you'll send a fresh pack of crayons if she calls you within the week.

- Try a more humorous approach with a teenager. Write a note that says, "Caller number one will receive a free autographed picture of Uncle Enrique the Great."

Little details like these will make it clear that you genuinely want to talk with a young person—and listen, of course! Adding a little extra something will break the ice and make your caller more comfortable.

* * * * *

To find the least-expensive calling cards, compare prices at discount stores such as Costco and Target, and watch for sales. If you can afford more than one card when you find a good price, buy several to stock up for the future.

Send a Forwarding Address

Linda Schulzetenberg says that it seems like a thousand years ago that she was teaching first grade as "Miss Garrison" in Avon, Minnesota. She was 22 years old at the time. At the end of the 1981–1982 school year, she gave her students her home address and invited them to write to her.

One of her students, Laura, was a little girl with saucer-shaped eyes and a round face. She took this invitation seriously and began writing letters to her former teacher. In the meantime, Linda got married, had children, and moved to Wisconsin, then to California, and eventually back to Minnesota. Linda was always careful to send Laura her new address, but somewhere along the way her former student stopped writing back. Linda figured that perhaps it wasn't cool for a teenager to write to her first-grade teacher.

Then one summer day, Linda received a thick envelope with a familiar return address. Laura, now 27 years old, had invited Linda to her wedding. Although she was planning to attend another wedding on the same day, Linda split her time between the two events to be sure that she'd get to see her former student again. This fond reunion rekindled their friendship, and they continue to stay in touch to this day.

Looking back at the experience, Linda says, "My advice to adults is to *always* make sure that any child who was special to you has your updated postal address. Even if you haven't heard from that person for years, if you move, send a postcard or the like and inform that person of your change of address, Who knows? You may also receive a thick envelope inviting you to one of life's most significant events."

* * * * *

For information about forwarding mail in the United States, stop by your local post office or visit movers-guide.usps.com on the Internet. For information about forwarding mail in Canada, visit www.canadapost.ca/personal/.

Recorded Reading

When I was a little girl, my brother and I shared a portable record player. I remember cleaning the needle before starting the record that went with our Cinderella book. I already knew how to read to myself, but there was something strangely thrilling about following along with the recorded voice. I still distinctly recall the sound of the harp that signaled it was time to turn the page.

Now instead of records there are cassette tapes, CDs, and iPods®. But no matter the format, children will always love interactive recorded stories. And what could be better than hearing the voice of Mommy while she is on a business trip, or the voice of a favorite uncle who lives 2,000 miles away?

All you need is a recording device, a picture book for young children or chapter book for older kids and teens, and a noise to indicate that it is time to turn the page. (Simply tapping a fork against a glass will do.) Many great books can be bought cheaply at used book stores. If you cannot afford to purchase the book, ask your local librarian to recommend a story that the child will likely be able to obtain at a public library. Start your recording with a greeting and a few words about the book you have chosen. Read at a moderate pace with a loud, clear voice to allow the child to follow along as you read.

For older children and teenagers, try reading an age-appropriate book with many chapters and sending one recorded chapter each week or month. Some teenagers may be ready to read the same books you enjoy; instead of recording the book itself, record your own thoughts about each chapter, making the experience into a remote book club. For adolescents who don't enjoy reading very much, this activity may be just the thing to spark their interest.

You can't force kids to love reading, but you can set an example by showing how much it means to you. Anything you do to make reading more fun and more personal is a step in the right direction.

· · · · ·

If you'd like help selecting books for kids from early childhood through high school, see the revised and updated third edition of The New York Times Parent's Guide to the Best Books for Children *by Eden Ross Lipson (Three Rivers Press, 2000).*

Ask for a New Picture

Kristin Johnstad's job in Minnesota frequently takes her on the road and away from her 4-year-old daughter, Ella. Kristin always leaves behind notes and calls often during her trips. In addition to the consistent communication during her absence, she and Ella prepare for the separation by selecting a new photo for Kristin to take on her trip before each departure.

Ella is the one who chooses the photo, but they both talk about her choice and why she selected that particular one. Ella tells her mom what she wants her to think about when she looks at the photo. Kristin uses the photo as a bookmark and sets it on the nightstand in her hotel room.

Since some kids love to sketch pictures and others feel self-conscious about their appearance, one variation on this idea is to ask the young person to draw a self-portrait. Requesting a drawing allows you to show your dedication while respecting their preferences. Another option is to request a themed collage, or a picture with a hidden message. Your job will be to figure out the theme or message and report back to the young person when you return.

Even if you live far away and don't see a child regularly, this is an easy idea to adapt. You can ask for a new picture whenever you get together, but you need not wait for a face-to-face visit. Send a stamped, self-addressed envelope with a request for a recent photograph or drawing. Include a brief note explaining why you want one and asking the child to explain why he or she chose a particular image. The next time you host your young friend in your home, be sure the latest picture is displayed in a prominent location.

• • • • •

Some families don't take many photographs, and it may be difficult for a child to send them frequently. Stay in touch with a parent or caregiver to find out when they have school photos to share.

Same Time, Same Channel

Television viewing is controversial ground in the world of child-rearing. Some adults see educational programming as a valuable learning tool. Others think that no TV is good TV. Whether the concern is quality control or quantity control, many people share some disdain for the programs that are now available to children and youth during prime-time viewing.

Your opinions about a child's television habits may be especially frustrating when you live far away. Instead of worrying helplessly, why not invite a young person to watch a show together? You could ask her or him to recommend a favorite show, or you could make several age-appropriate suggestions and have the young person choose. Once you've both settled on a show, schedule a time to call on the phone and watch it at the same time; if your time zones are far apart, make a plan to talk after the program has aired in both places.

Try not to make this into a lecture or opportunity to demonstrate how "cool" you are; most kids can see through your outward show if you are actually being judgmental or insincere. Instead, use the program to learn more about your young friend. Try asking some of these questions:

- Who is your favorite character on the show?

- Would you change the ending of the program? How?

- Do you have friends who watch this show, too?

Always wait until a commercial break or the end of the show to start a deeper conversation, or you're not likely to get much of a response.

Remember that kids may not always like the same things you like, but don't make assumptions about them, either. You may be surprised to learn that your 6-year-old niece is already a sports fanatic, or your 13-year-old grandson happens to love watching nature shows.

• • • • •

If you know a kid who doesn't watch television (either by choice or because caregivers don't allow it), find out what other kinds of media they enjoy. You may be able to read the same magazines, rent the same movies, or tune into a favorite radio station using a Web site that offers a Webcast.

Talk Every Day

Thanks to cell phones, calling cards, and competition between telephone companies, the price of a long-distance call is becoming more affordable all the time. You can use your pocket change or your "free" minutes to be a consistent voice in a young person's life.

Daily conversation topics can cover virtually anything you both share an interest in. An older kid may have fun trying to answer a trivia question each day, or perhaps you can each share the worst thing and the best thing that happened that day. Some children might enjoy hearing science facts about their favorite animals, and teenagers may be interested in discussing the day's news headlines.

It can be daunting to come up with a new conversation every day, so it is best to keep the daily check-in fairly brief. Short and somewhat structured contact ensures that you both get to talk without running out of things to say. A young child may enjoy setting an egg timer that makes a noise at the end of your chat.

You may also want to add to the ritual by calling or

e-mailing at approximately the same time every day. You could call to share in a brief prayer or blessing before a meal, for example. If you know a sports fan, the two of you could send instant messages online immediately following the sports segment of the nightly news.

Joanne McQuiggan of Waterloo, Ontario, keeps daily contact with her young children, Sam and Nicole, by reading them a bedtime story every night, no matter how far away they are. Joanne's work takes her to many different places across Canada and around the world, but she always takes the same item on every trip: an anthology of children's stories. Her children keep a copy of the anthology at home. Every night while Joanne's away, her husband helps the children choose one story from the anthology. This way, when Sam and Nicole call their mom for a bedtime story, Joanne can read the story over the phone as the kids follow along.

Communicating every day may sound pretty ambitious for an aunt, grandparent, or friend, but some long-distance parents swear by it. One father said, "Even if I only get to talk to my son for two minutes a day, at least he knows that I'm thinking about him all the time."

• ◦ • ◦

Check out Conversations on the Go *by Mary Acker-man (Search Institute, 2004) to find additional questions and tips for talking with young people. For daily information about specific interests, try purchasing a themed desk calendar from a local bookstore.*

Joint Journaling

Megan Myers works at the United States embassy in Ulaan-baatar, Mongolia. She has lived and traveled all over the world, but she still remembers how nervous she felt when she first left home to live in another country. When she was 16 years old, she spent a year as a foreign exchange student in France. She felt lonely and overwhelmed at first, but she found it helpful to write in a journal. By the end of her stay in France, Megan had filled several books with her reflections on the experience.

Megan's younger sister, Margit, decided to travel to Germany a few years later during her own high-school years. Recalling the difficulty of relocating by herself at that age, Megan offered her journals to Margit. Margit began reading the first installment on the plane, and it was a chance for her to see that her fears and worries were entirely normal.

If you kept journals when you were young and don't mind revealing them to another person, consider sharing them with someone who is at the same stage in life. Did you ever write about going to a new school, or trying out for a sports team, or getting in a fight with a friend, or asking someone on a date? Your childhood excitement, doubts, successes, and problems may help a young person feel closer to you. Even if some of your writing seems silly or embarrassing now, it might actually be fun to discuss with a young person who is facing some similar experiences.

If you didn't write in a journal when you were growing up, you might consider starting a shared journal with your young friend. When Rachel Mason left for college in Washington, D.C., she wanted to keep in touch with a friend back home in Minnesota. The two of them took turns writing in a single journal. They mailed the book back and forth, each person adding several paragraphs of anecdotes or questions. When they filled up the journal, they had a great keepsake of their friendship during that time.

A journal is a private, intimate document. By sharing your innermost thoughts with a young person, you can establish a level of trust and friendship that is difficult to attain through conversations alone.

• • • • •

Consider purchasing and decorating a journal while you are together during a visit. Even if the two of you just glue magazine images to the cover of an inexpensive notebook, it will give your journal a personal touch.

Calendar Countdown

Shveta Thakrar of Edison, New Jersey, spent a year in Germany as a student when she was in college. When she returned to the United States, her new European friends were great about keeping in touch by sending surprises and letters. She was delighted to receive an Adventskalendar, which Germans use to count down the days of Advent leading up to Christmas.

Similar calendar traditions exist in other countries, but the German version usually includes a little door to open each day, with a trinket or a piece of chocolate hidden behind every door. Shveta's friends created a different version that was tailored to her love of reading. They strung together envelopes, and each day she opened a quote, a poem, or an excerpt from a story. One of her favorites was a German poem called *Einhorn* ("Unicorn") by Hilde Domin; she still has her copy of this treasured poem.

You need not celebrate a religious holiday to adapt this tradition in your own relationship. Any countdown will do, and you can select gifts that are relevant for whichever event you choose. Think creatively about the possibilities:

- Send pencils and other supplies to count down the days until school starts.

- Send encouraging stickers (with phrases like "Good luck!" or "You can do it!") to count down to a big game or a recital.

- Send small party decorations to count down to the young person's birthday.

- Send key chains, a wallet, a gasoline debit card, and sunglasses to count down to the day when a teenager gets a driver's license.

- Send photos and postcards to count down the days until your next visit together.

Even if you send just seven envelopes with notes or cartoons inside, you'll succeed in building anticipation for a whole week.

When you've gathered your countdown materials, label each item with a date. As you pack them up, be sure to include instructions to open only one each day.

• • • • •

Watch for calendar sales in January and February. You can find some dramatic discounts after the first of the year, and it may be inexpensive to purchase a special calendar to be used in your countdown later in the year.

Share Your Music

Chad Mathis was only 4 years old when his older brother Dan left for college in 1991. Dan had spent his high-school years baby-sitting and playing with Chad in Watford City, North Dakota; now, he worried that his little brother would forget him or grow apart from him. Dan was determined to remain close to Chad no matter where he lived.

One of Dan's main interests is music, so when Chad was about 6 years old, Dan taped a mix of funny songs for him. The older brother didn't realize it at the time, but that tape forged a new bond between the two. Chad listened to the songs incessantly and grew particularly fond of the band They Might Be Giants. Later, when Chad was 13 years old, Dan took him to see this favorite band in Minneapolis, Minnesota, in 1999. Chad flew to stay with his big brother in New York City and saw the band again at Central Park in 2002.

Chad's musical tastes did expand over the years. Dan continued to give Chad new music, and he was always careful to choose not only the songs and albums that *he* liked best, but also the ones he thought Chad would like. Dan included notes describing why he thought Chad might be interested in various performers. The two of them now share a love of The Beach Boys, Nirvana, The White Stripes, and other bands. As Chad prepares to head off to college himself, the two brothers are closer than ever.

Kids have the capacity to like all kinds of music. Don't worry about being out of touch with "what the kids are listening to these days." Whether you like Carole King or Outkast, taking the time to share your music—and listen to their music—is a fantastic way to start conversations and potentially identify common interests.

● ● ● ● ●

Dan recommends www.allmusic.com as a great Web site for researching popular music. If you know a young person's favorite bands or artists, you can search this site by performer or by genre to help explore her or his interests.

Blog Together

If you and your young friend are both computer users, blogging may be the perfect way to stay connected. The word *blog* is short for *Web log,* and it refers to an online method of communication that a person or a group of people can use to share ideas. You can create a blog on a free Web site, use it to post ongoing commentary, and then control who has access to the Web site. Other readers can respond by posting comments of their own on particular blog entries.

Blogs take many forms. Some people use them simply as a diary, and they may not invite anyone to read what they've written. Others use their blogs to promote political views or religious beliefs. Families or groups of friends might use a blog to keep in touch with each other on a daily, weekly, or monthly basis.

You may want to set up a blog, or you may invite a savvy young person to set one up for the two of you. Using this format is a nice change from regular e-mail for several reasons. For one thing, the novelty of an "official" Web site might appeal to kids. A blog also acts as a single archive of your communication over a long period of time. Because you establish a private place for this interaction, you may develop a heightened sense of trust between the two of you.

If a young person is not interested in this kind of blogging, encourage setting up her or his own Web site. Check the site frequently and give positive feedback about the content or the design.

● ● ● ● ●

For more information about starting a blog, visit www.blogger.com. For tips about ensuring safe use of the Internet for minors, visit www.safekids.com or www.safeteens.com.

Remembered Recipes

When I moved out of the dorms for my third year of college, I knew how to prepare four foods: JELL-O®, deviled eggs, scrambled eggs, and macaroni and cheese from a box. Not a promising menu, huh? I was delighted later that year when my Aunt Taryn gave me a personal recipe book for Christmas. It included some of my favorites from her repertoire and several blank cards that I could use to add recipes of my own.

When my younger brother and cousins graduated from high school, I adapted this idea and made recipe boxes for them. I decorated the outside with pictures of food, and I used index cards to write down several favorite recipes. I included some of the same ones Taryn had given me, and I also added recipes I had received from our grandma and my dad. I cannot imagine these particular boys making pie crust, but I hope each of the different family recipes will bring them back to a kitchen filled with laughter and mouth-watering aromas.

Even if you are trying to connect with a younger child, you can start this tradition early. File away each treasured recipe as you learn which dishes the child likes best. You may prefer to keep the book or box at your home until graduation day, or you may think the child is already mature enough to be interested in it.

Before completing the recipe collection, you might ask other adults in the child's life to contribute their own ideas. Gathering input from others will make your gift even more meaningful when he or she is ready to move beyond macaroni and cheese.

●　●　●　●　●

Each year on the child's birthday, ask for and write down a list of her or his favorite foods to keep with the recipe collection. It will be fun to look back and see how tastes have changed or stayed the same over the years.

Uphold a Yearly Ritual

Several of the ideas in this book can become rituals through repetition, but creating a formal tradition can be especially fun for young people, particularly if you only see a child once or twice a year.

When you have a flexible travel budget and plenty of vacation time, it is easy to schedule a yearly activity; however, many loved ones are only able to see each other infrequently during holidays, spring breaks, or summer trips. Plan your ritual around whatever time you have together:

- Hold a dreidel tournament during Chanukah.

- Let your young relative pick out the turkey for Thanksgiving dinner.

- Make green eggs and ham on St. Patrick's Day.

- Go fishing (or ice fishing!) on New Year's Eve.

- If one of you lives in a town or city with a local celebration, get together to watch the parade or attend the coronation of the town's "royalty."

- Bake Christmas cookies together on December 23rd.

- Watch fireworks together on Canada Day or the 4th of July.

- Make May Day baskets and deliver them to neighbors on May 1st.

Sometimes you simply can't be together at the same time every year. If that's the case, choose a tradition that you can observe even when you are apart:

- Step outside and look at the new crescent moon at the beginning of Ramadan.

- Have a contest to send the most creative homemade card on Valentine's Day.

- Simultaneously light candles to celebrate the life of a deceased loved one on Día de los Muertos (Day of the Dead).

- Plant one tree each on Earth Day.

Your ritual does not have to be religious, political, or philosophical—it simply has to be *yours*. The act of repeating it is enough to make it meaningful. When you decide to observe a tradition with a young person, the two of you will have a whole string of memories to enjoy.

• • • • •

Give your tradition room for flexibility. Your opportunities and resources may change over time, and it is not necessary to make the ritual exactly the same on every occasion. For example, if a teenager is no longer interested in flying a kite on the first day of spring, consider researching and flying model airplanes instead.

Stick with Them

Jennifer Johnson grew up in the very small town of Hendrum, Minnesota, and almost everyone she loved lived nearby. She does remember one rare visit from her father's friend, Jim, who he met in the Navy. Jim brought his girlfriend with him, and "Miss Dorothy" took a shine to Jennifer and her younger sister, Jessica. The girls were very young, and they were quite impressed when this friendly stranger kept in touch with them even after she and Jim broke up a year later.

Throughout their childhood, Miss Dorothy would send gifts and letters. She always remembered them on their birthdays and at Christmas. She sent some of their favorite stuffed animals, and she crocheted homemade blankets for them. They wrote thank-you letters back to their "phantom" auntie. Jennifer remembers thinking, "There's this lady in Maryland who loves us for some reason." She still doesn't even remember what Miss Dorothy looked like.

Twenty-five years later, Jennifer still has her blanket, and she still feels loved by this mysterious woman. Although

Miss Dorothy had no obligations—no ties to them whatso-
ever—she continually remembered the girls, who are now
grown women. She even sent Jennifer a gift for her wedding.

You don't have to be a relative to change the life of a
child. You don't have to be invited, and you don't have to
have a reason. Just giving yourself in a consistent and caring
way is enough to make a tremendous impact.

• • • • •

*If you know you want to remain committed to a child
or a teenager for several years, create a joint time
capsule. Make plans to open it together in 1, 5, or 10
years.*

Don't Stop Now!

There are many other ways to keep in touch across the miles, including:

- If you have access to a fax machine, invite a young person to fax her or his homework assignments to you. Use this as a way to help with project ideas or to check for completion.

- Watch the skies together. Learn about constellations, comets, and eclipses, and see if you can spot the same phenomena from your two locations.

- Choose a special song, and call each other every time you hear it.

- Purchase two subscriptions (one for each of you) to a magazine that interests you both. Point out the articles you enjoy, and ask which ones the young person likes best.

- Celebrate "graduation day" at the end of every grade. Send the young person a homemade diploma and a letter of congratulations.

FREQUENTLY ASKED QUESTIONS

-or-

What to remember when a long-distance relationship with a young person seems too hard

What if my efforts aren't appreciated?

As this book took shape, many adults expressed concern to me that their efforts would mean nothing, that their gestures would go unnoticed. But take a moment to think of three adults who mattered to you when you were young. (Try to think of at least one adult who lived far away.) How did you show your gratitude? Did you write lengthy letters to Grandpa, telling him he made you feel valued and respected? Did you tell your mother's college friend her annual gifts of art supplies provided hours of creative fun? Did you tell your divorced father you spent all week looking forward to his Sunday phone calls?

You may have shared these feelings as an adult, but chances are you were less forthcoming as a child or a teenager. Kids can be shy around adults, especially those they rarely see in person. A boy may grunt yes-and-no answers over the phone as you discuss world travel, only to turn around and brag to his friends about his aunt's trip to Africa. A teenage girl may sound bored or timid as she says a forced thank-you for the book you sent, but that book may be the one that inspires her to write her first novel.

The point is, if you are hoping for an outpouring of gratitude and long, heartfelt conversations, you may be disappointed. Some kids will lavish praise and love on their favorite adults, and some simply won't. That doesn't mean your efforts are worthless. Keep in mind that a decade may pass before your niece realizes how much you contributed to her love of music, and your grandson may not appreciate that book of family recipes until he has a family of his own. Even if the results aren't immediately apparent, your love and attention are still the most valuable gifts you can offer. Give them freely.

I am too nervous to talk to teenagers. What if they reject me?

Fear of rejection is a common obstacle adults face in connecting with young people—especially teenagers. In her book *Tag, You're It!* (Search Institute, 2004) Kathleen Kimball-Baker describes her experience of interviewing several teenagers to learn more about the adult relationships in their lives. She was inspired to discover that they truly *do* want more adults to care about them and build relationships with them.

Think about the way you interacted with adults who touched your life when you were a teenager. Did you ever shrug at their questions, blush furiously at their compliments, or ignore their suggestions? These are just a few of the behaviors you may encounter. Despite their outward actions, research reveals teens want adults to trust them, to spend time with them, and to be their friends.

In his book *WHY Do They Act That Way?* (Free Press, 2004), clinical psychologist David Walsh shows how teen brain development affects their behaviors. You may be worried about having to deal with mood swings, communication problems, or risky activities. Dr. Walsh's research shows that these are actually normal, physical responses to brain growth.

Once you know that teens really need you in their lives and cannot help some of their impulsive reactions, it is much easier to tolerate their silences or eye rolling. You don't have to be cool to make a difference. You just have to be dedicated.

What if the parents resent my attempts to be involved?

While most parents will welcome support from other caring adults, it is possible your efforts will not initially be welcome. Maybe you haven't spoken to your ex-spouse since your divorce, or perhaps you have a hard time getting along with your son- or daughter-in-law. In these delicate situations, it is important to set your differences aside and find common ground.

Even if you have your own feelings of anger or resentment, try to take a positive approach. Say something like, "I know it is difficult to take care of a family, and I really think your daughter/son is great. I would love to spend some time getting to know her/him." If you have a specific gesture in mind, ask about it in advance: "I was thinking I might send a CD that I recorded. Is that okay?" Consulting with parents or caregivers up front shows you respect their authority, which may reduce the likelihood of future problems.

YMCA of the USA and Search Institute conducted a 2002 poll of 1,005 adults. This poll found that most parents feel they are "going it alone." Parents may not feel comfortable asking for your involvement, but they can certainly benefit from it (Roelhkepartain et al. 2002).

Please note that states and provinces have varied laws about child visitation rights for parents, grandparents, foster parents, and stepparents. If you have trouble reaching an agreement with a young person's caregiver but feel strongly that you should be a part of that child's life, seek advice from a lawyer, a family mediator, or a nonprofit organization that works with families.

Reference

Roelhkepartain, E.C., Scales, P.C., Roehlkepartain, J.L., Gallo, C., & Rude, S.P. (2002). *Building strong families: Highlights from a preliminary survey from YMCA of the USA and Search Institute on what parents need to succeed.* YMCA of the USA and Search Institute. (Download this report by visiting the "Families" section on www.search-institute.org/research/publications.html)

What if I disagree with the way the parent or caregiver is raising this child?

As an adult, perhaps you have identified some of the "flaws" of your childhood. Maybe you think your parents were crazy to let you spend afternoons alone in junior high, or you cringe when you remember your steady diet of junk food through elementary school. Your caregivers may have made a few errors in judgment, but you still managed to become the caring individual reading this book today. Isn't it possible that a child whose parent you don't see eye-to-eye with will *also* grow to become a great adult?

Try to keep this question in mind when you feel compelled to criticize a parent's child-rearing technique. Before rushing to make a suggestion, take a step back and ask yourself, "How will the parent's decision affect this child in 30 years?" Obviously negligent or abusive behavior is unacceptable and may have serious effects on a young person well into adulthood; in this case, you are right to intervene. Preschool clothing styles, on the other hand, are not likely to ruin a child permanently. There will always be gray areas, of course. For example, what exactly constitutes "educational" television, and what effects will viewing habits have in the long run?

Even though your heart is in the right place, unless you are a parent with partial custody, it is probably best to refrain from being critical as much as possible. The parent or caregiver is your ally in building this relationship, and the child will suffer if the two of you are at odds.

What if I am way behind on technology? I don't know the first thing about computers, video cameras, or cell phones!

Some of the ideas in this book involve technology, but very few are dependent on it. If blogging and online gaming are completely foreign concepts to you, there's no need to feel inadequate. You may make a far bigger impact with a thoughtful package or a series of fun postcards.

Some kids have a DVD player in every room (and in the car!), and you may be amazed when you see a young person playing an elaborate video game on a tiny cell phone. Remember that even technology becomes boring with repetition. Your handmade journal or instant picnic may seem refreshing and far more interesting than an e-mail message.

What could a young person and I possibly have in common?

Your existing connection to this young person is an obvious starting point. Maybe you are family members who can swap funny stories about relatives. Maybe you have known her or his parents for years and can shed some light on their personality quirks.

Remember that young people—even *very* young people—are just that: people. Some like music, or cars, or game shows. Some figure skate, some sing well, and others play football. Some love to be the center of attention, others enjoy reading quietly at the library, and still others feel as if they don't have a friend in the world.

It isn't necessary to like everything they like. You may disagree about hairstyles and television shows, and you may not know quite what to say to a 6-year-old. The goal is to pay attention and learn something about them. You'll be surprised at the amount of common ground you'll be able to uncover.

7

I hardly ever get to see this person. Why bother going to all of this trouble?

When you look back at your childhood or your teen years, you probably remember a few definitive moments or experiences. Maybe a teacher complimented your writing, or a neighbor complained to your parents about your fast driving. A few words uttered in a single moment can last forever in someone's memory.

When the distance seems discouraging, remind yourself that words and actions *do* make a difference for a young person. Initiating a caring, supportive relationship has the potential to change life's trajectory in dozens of positive ways. Your annual tradition of attending a concert together may start a lifelong love of music, or the letters you send may offer tremendous comfort and hope to a teenager who has few friends. You may not see an immediate payoff, but the investment is worthwhile in the long run.

I have trouble keeping in touch with people consistently. Should I start a long-distance relationship with a young person if I can only do it occasionally?

Yes! Young people do need consistent attention from adults, but frequent contact is not the only way to demonstrate your level of commitment. The sincerity of your messages and the quality of your gestures can be equally valuable.

The important thing here is to communicate your love, interest, and concern for the young person's well-being. If you have trouble staying in touch on a regular basis, decide that you will write one long, thoughtful letter every year on the child's birthday. Or, if you don't have the time or inclination to sit down and write, record your voice on an audio tape; if you have a difficult time remembering birthdays, add to the recording periodically and mail a tape after several months' worth of messages.

If you are prone to fleeting moments of guilt about not keeping in touch, transform those moments into meaningful gestures by starting a "Thinking of You" box or notebook. Jot down a quick sentence or two about whatever brought your young friend to mind. These may be very simple thoughts: "I saw a commercial for your favorite television show, and it made me laugh when I remembered your impression of the main character," or, "I made those cookies you loved so much when you visited last winter, and I was wishing you were here to enjoy them with me." You can read the messages when you get together, or send a batch once you have accumulated several.

ABOUT THE ASSETS

The Developmental Assets framework was first introduced in 1990. At that time, Search Institute identified and measured 30 Developmental Assets.

Search Institute continued to review the research and conduct studies, cumulatively surveying more than 350,000 students in grades 6 through 12 between 1990 and 1995. The surveys revealed the Developmental Assets they experienced, the risks they took, the deficits they had to overcome, and the ways they thrived. The institute also conducted numerous informal discussions and focus groups. As a result of these ongoing research activities, in 1996 the Developmental Assets framework was revised into its current form, a model of 40 Developmental Assets for adolescents.

What follows is Search Institute's list of 40 Developmental Assets for Adolescents (ages 12–18). The institute continues its long-term research efforts to refine, measure, and test the asset frameworks for children of all ages. For free, downloadable asset lists in French and Spanish, and for different age groups, please visit www.search-institute. org/assets.

Search Institute has identified the following building blocks of healthy development that help young people grow up healthy, caring, and responsible.

EXTERNAL ASSETS

SUPPORT

1. **Family support**—Family life provides high levels of love and support.

2. **Positive family communication**—Young person and her or his parent(s) communicate positively, and young person is willing to seek advice and counsel from parents.

3. **Other adult relationships**—Young person receives support from three or more nonparent adults.

4. **Caring neighborhood**—Young person experiences caring neighbors.

5. **Caring school climate**—School provides a caring, encouraging environment.

6. **Parent involvement in schooling**—Parent(s) are actively involved in helping young person succeed in school.

EMPOWERMENT

7. **Community values youth**—Young person perceives that adults in the community value youth.

8. **Youth as resources**—Young people are given useful roles in the community.

9. **Service to others**—Young person serves in the community one hour or more per week.

10. **Safety**—Young person feels safe at home, at school, and in the neighborhood.

EXTERNAL ASSETS

BOUNDARIES AND EXPECTATIONS

11. **Family boundaries**—Family has clear rules and consequences and monitors the young person's whereabouts.

12. **School boundaries**—School provides clear rules and consequences.

13. **Neighborhood boundaries**—Neighbors take responsibility for monitoring young people's behavior.

14. **Adult role models**—Parent(s) and other adults model positive, responsible behavior.

15. **Positive peer influence**—Young person's best friends model responsible behavior.

16. **High expectations**—Both parent(s) and teachers encourage the young person to do well.

CONSTRUCTIVE USE OF TIME

17. **Creative activities**—Young person spends three or more hours per week in lessons or practice in music, theater, or other arts.

18. **Youth programs**—Young person spends three or more hours per week in sports, clubs, or organizations at school and/or in the community.

19. **Religious community**—Young person spends one or more hours per week in activities in a religious institution.

20. **Time at home**—Young person is out with friends "with nothing special to do" two or fewer nights per week.

INTERNAL ASSETS

COMMITMENT TO LEARNING

21. Achievement motivation—Young person is motivated to do well in school.

22. School engagement—Young person is actively engaged in learning.

23. Homework—Young person reports doing at least one hour of homework every school day.

24. Bonding to school—Young person cares about her or his school.

25. Reading for pleasure—Young person reads for pleasure three or more hours per week.

POSITIVE VALUES

26. Caring—Young person places high value on helping other people.

27. Equality and social justice—Young person places high value on promoting equality and reducing hunger and poverty.

28. Integrity—Young person acts on convictions and stands up for her or his beliefs.

29. Honesty—Young person "tells the truth even when it is not easy."

30. Responsibility—Young person accepts and takes personal responsibility.

31. Restraint—Young person believes it is important not to be sexually active or to use alcohol or other drugs.

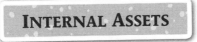

INTERNAL ASSETS

SOCIAL COMPETENCIES

32. Planning and decision making—Young person knows how to plan ahead and make choices.

33. Interpersonal competence—Young person has empathy, sensitivity, and friendship skills.

34. Cultural competence—Young person has knowledge of and comfort with people of different cultural/racial/ethnic backgrounds.

35. Resistance skills—Young person can resist negative peer pressure and dangerous situations.

36. Peaceful conflict resolution—Young person seeks to resolve conflict nonviolently.

POSITIVE IDENTITY

37. Personal power—Young person feels he or she has control over "things that happen to me."

38. Self-esteem—Young person reports having a high self-esteem.

39. Sense of purpose—Young person reports that "my life has a purpose."

40. Positive view of personal future—Young person is optimistic about her or his personal future.

ADDITIONAL SEARCH INSTITUTE RESOURCES

150 Ways to Show Kids You Care (Los Niños Importan: 150 Maneras de Demostrárselo). Even the simplest acts of kindness can build assets in the lives of children. This warm, inviting, bilingual book provides 150 easy ideas and meaningful reminders about how adults can show kids they really care.

"Ask Me Where I'm Going" & Other Revealing Messages from Today's Teens. This intimate little book will touch your heart as you read poignant and practical "real words" from teens describing what they really want from the caring adults in their lives.

Conversations on the Go: Clever Questions to Keep Teens and Grown-Ups Talking by Mary Ackerman. This stimulating book gives teens and adults a chance to find out what the other one thinks. Filled with intriguing questions, some deep and some just fun, it's guaranteed to stretch the imagination and bring out each other's personality and true self.

Just When I Needed You: True Stories of Adults Who Made a Difference in the Lives of Young People written and edited by Deborah Fischer. *Just When I Needed You* is a hope-filled collection of stories from adults who remember the people that were there for them when they were growing up, and how they grew up to make an impact on the young people they know today.

Playful Reading: Positive, Fun Ways to Build the Bond Between Preschoolers, Books, and You by Carolyn Munson-Benson. *Playful Reading* takes readers on a joyful romp through asset-rich children's picture books, emphasizing early literacy skills, reading for pleasure, and the eight asset categories. The book comes full of activities, discussion topics, and ways to create memorable moments between children and the adults who read to them.

Tag, You're It! 50 Easy Ways to Connect with Young People by Kathleen Kimball-Baker. This motivating book offers commonsense ideas to connect and build assets with young people. Youth workers, parents, educators, business people, congregation leaders, and anyone who cares about youth will love this book. The *Tag, You're It!* card deck and the *Tag, You're It!* posters are also specifically designed to spark conversations between youth and adults.

Who, Me? Surprisingly Doable Ways You Can Make a Difference for Kids. Use this desktop perpetual calendar for reminders, tips, and inspiration in your daily interactions with kids and teens. Here you'll find great, concrete asset-building ideas from dozens of the best Search Institute youth publications.

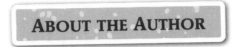

ABOUT THE AUTHOR

Tenessa Gemelke has worked and volunteered for many years in recreation centers, youth clubs, library programs, and mentoring programs. She was also a contributing writer for *Building Assets Is Elementary: Group Activities for Helping Kids Ages 8-12 Succeed.* Gemelke is currently an associate editor at Search Institute and has edited several resources on positive youth development, including *Who, Me? Surprisingly Doable Ways You Can Make a Difference for Kids* and *The Journey of Community Change.* She lives in Minneapolis, Minnesota with her husband and son.

ABOUT SEARCH INSTITUTE

Search Institute is an independent nonprofit organization whose mission is to provide leadership, knowledge, and resources to promote healthy children, youth, and communities. To accomplish this mission, the Institute generates and communicates new knowledge, and brings together community, state, and national leaders. For a free information packet, call 800-888-7828 or visit our Web site at www.search-institute.org.